THE REAL McCOY

BIRTHDAY
PRESENT

FROM

RICHARD &
MARIE.

The Real McCoy

My Life So Far

Tony McCoy with Claude Duval

CORONET BOOKS
Hodder and Stoughton

First published in Great Britain in 1998 by
Hodder and Stoughton
a division of Hodder Headline PLC

A Coronet paperback

10 9 8 7 6 5 4 3 2 1

ISBN: 0 340 69682 6

Typeset by Hewer Text Ltd, Edinburgh
Printed and bound in Great Britain by
Mackays of Chatham PLC

Hodder and Stoughton
A Division of Hodder Headline PLC
338 Euston Road
London NW1 3BH

Contents

Acknowledgements

My thanks to my mother and father and all my family in Northern Ireland, and the many other owners and trainers who have been behind me all the way. Also to my fellow jockeys, whose camaraderie is second to none. I should also like to mention the countless brave horses, without whose courageous efforts I would not have been able to make so many dreams come true in such a short time. Finally I should like to thank my friend Claude Duval for his invaluable help with the writing of the book.

Photographic Acknowledgements
For permission to reproduce copyright photographs, the author and publisher would like to thank the following: Edward Whitaker, Gerry Cranham, Pat Healy, Caroline Norris, Phil Smith, Dan Abraham, Philippa Gilchrist, *The Sun*.

Publishers note
Tony McCoy's first-person narrative is interspersed with comments and quotes from people who have played an important role in his life-story so far.

Foreword

I am glad I retired in 1985 . . . it means I never had to ride against Tony McCoy. No praise is too high for the young Irishman and his gripping autobiography comes to life when you read just how much he has achieved in such a short time.

I rode 1,138 winners from 1970 to 1985, including seven championship titles, but in just three seasons in England Tony has already ridden 439 winners. Barring accidents, he will surely beat Peter Scudamore's record of 1,678 winners, achieved between 1978 and 1993, and become the most successful jump jockey of all time.

I've seen films of the great Fred Winter in action, although jumping has changed so much since those days. I rode against Jonjo O'Neill, Peter Scudamore and Richard Dunwoody, who were all mighty hard to beat, but Tony McCoy is as good as any of them already. Six times a day, six or seven days a week, Tony gives all his rides a chance to win. He never seems to give up, and I've seen him win on horses who have no right to be in the winners' enclosure.

Tony has pulled countless little races out of the fire, but his Cheltenham Gold Cup win in 1997 on Mr Mulligan was quite superb. He made a very difficult ride look so very easy.

Like myself, Tony never smokes or drinks. Perhaps he also realises that the career span of a jump jockey is quite short and you have to take advantage of every opportunity that comes your way. Tony may be champion for many years to come with a balanced mind and body.

Tony's career has been pure magic, and I've enjoyed reading this account of it. The title of 'The World's Greatest Jockey' given to me by John McCririck, is in great danger!

JOHN FRANCOME

Introduction

The Real McCoy – I used to think that if I see that title in a headline again I will scream; but I suppose I can't really blame the sub-editors. It's a natural headline and I have to admit that my career as a jockey has been a fairytale. I often have to pinch myself to believe that so much has happened to me in such a short time.

When Make A Stand won the Sun King of the Punters Lanzarote Handicap Hurdle at Kempton on 18 January 1997, it equalled the biggest previous win of my career, which came a year earlier when I won the same race on Warm Spell at 20–1 for trainer Gary Moore. I was also fortunate enough to win on Viking Flagship, Top Spin and Zabadi at Aintree in 1996.

Although I was champion jockey in the 1995–6 season, it was pointed out that I had not really won any of the big races. However, after my last-fence fall on Mr Mulligan in the King George VI Chase at Kempton on Boxing Day 1996, I enjoyed a dream run, kicked off by Make A Stand at Kempton. Beyond my wildest dreams, Make A Stand and Mr Mulligan went on to win the Champion Hurdle and Gold Cup at Cheltenham.

The one blimp came when the Jockey Club's medical officials insisted that I was unable to ride Belmont King in the Martell Grand National. After a fall at Uttoxeter I was told that I had been banned from riding on medical grounds for ten days. They then changed their minds and extended the ban to twenty-one days, thus wrecking my dream of being only the second jockey ever to pull off the treble of the Champion Hurdle, Gold Cup and Grand National in one season.

Here again Lady Luck smiled on me, however: Belmont King was pulled out of the rearranged National on the Monday after Saturday's IRA bomb scare, and I was back in action and able to ride him to victory in the Scottish Grand National two weeks later.

For a few strides after the Pond fence at Sandown in April, I actually thought that I'd also win the Whitbread on Flyer's Nap, until he blundered at the last and I was beaten up the hill by one of Robert Alner's other runners Harwell Lad, ridden by thirty-seven-year-old amateur Rupert Nuttall.

I have been so lucky along the way. Back in Toomebridge in County Antrim I have wonderful parents in Peadar and Claire McCoy. My father always seemed to know that I would end up with a career in racing, allowing me to play truant and spend hours with trainer Billy Rock, when I should have been at school studying.

I was lucky to get a job with County Carlow flat trainer Jim Bolger. Jim is a hard man and a tough taskmaster, but he knocked me into shape, and I would not be where I am now without his help. Perhaps luck also came into it when I broke my leg: my weight shot up dramatically and I began to concentrate on a career as a jump jockey, although I upset Jim Bolger when I left for England.

Perhaps the best advice I was ever given came from Northern Ireland trainer–amateur rider Paddy Graffin, who told me when I was still with Jim Bolger, 'Get a one-way ticket to England . . . and don't come back.' It was hard leaving Jim Bolger, and to this day he thinks I deserted him too soon, but like myself, Aidan O'Brien and Paul Carberry have done quite well since leaving his stables.

Teaming up with Toby Balding was another stroke of luck. He and Kim Bailey are the only current jump trainers in England to have won the big three of the Champion Hurdle, Gold Cup and Grand National.

David Bridgwater's shock decision to quit as Martin Pipe's first jockey midway through the 1996–7 season was another bit of luck for me. If that had not happened I would not have had the chance to win the Champion Hurdle on Make A Stand. Staying freelance also paid dividends, however: if I had accepted Martin Pipe's offer to be his retained rider, I would not have been free to win the Gold Cup on Mr Mulligan, or the Scottish National on Belmont King. I intend to ride freelance for as long as I can, and hope that my agent Dave Roberts, who has played such a big part in my success, can keep all my trainers happy – no easy task.

My house move from Weyhill to Amesbury has taken me just ten miles down the road – 'Ten minutes closer to Martin Pipe,' joked one wag. I really want to stay as a freelance, though, and it would take a lot of money to get me tied down to any trainer, whether it was Martin Pipe or one of the other top men. I like the freedom to choose.

I broke Adrian Maguire's record of winners when I was champion conditional jockey in my first season in England with seventy-four winners, and was actually seventh in the overall list in the 1994–5 season. I was champion jockey in the 1995–6 season with 175 winners, and then again in 1996–7 with 190 winners. In three seasons I've now ridden 439 winners from 1,898 rides, a strike rate of twenty-three per cent. I am very much aware that riding in the hoofprints of Peter Scudamore and Richard Dunwoody as champion jockey is a great honour.

It has been a fairytale, and it just seems to be getting better and better, although there is still a great deal I would love to achieve. Riding 200 winners in a season and going on to beat Peter Scudamore's record of 221 is an obvious target. I believe that I might have managed this during the 1996–7 campaign but for injuries and suspensions which led to a total of eight weeks off. I also like to think that I would have ridden thirty-one winners in eight weeks to set a new record.

So much has been achieved in such a short time that it is almost a blur, and I haven't yet ridden at Carlisle, Newcastle or Catterick since I came to England.

Ascot is my favourite track because I have been lucky there, although I don't dislike the gaff tracks like Plumpton and Towcester. It is there that I often spot horses I'm not riding, and bear them in mind for a future occasion, when I might have the chance to ride them.

I have a dream every night that I will wake up in the morning, hop out of bed on to the scales which are always ready at my feet, and find that I am lighter . . . but it never happens and it never will. Being champion jockey has brought with it big financial rewards – in June 1997 I was able to buy a £200,000 country mansion just outside Amesbury in Wiltshire, literally a stone's throw from Stonehenge – but all the money in the world can't take pounds of weight off the scales for me, and I have to live on a near starvation diet.

I've tried the pee pills and they are dangerous. They make you feel giddy and can, in the end, make you put on more weight. I've even tried the old 'fingers down the throat' trick after a big meal, and that certainly does not work.

Being nearly six foot means that I am always going to have serious weight difficulties, and it is by far my biggest hang-up, as I love food, especially chops and steaks. After my fall at Uttoxeter when I was unconscious and consequently banned for twenty-one days, my weight went up from 9st 10lb to 11st 3lb because of the inactivity. I suppose if I had a desk job from nine to five and lived a pretty normal life I would weigh around eleven and a half stone. I can't believe that when I rode in my first race at Phoenix Park back in September 1990 I tipped the scales at 6st 4lb.

I realise that my success makes me very much public property when it comes to the betting fraternity. When Adrian Maguire rode a 355–1 five-timer at Kempton on 23 February 1997, Ladbroke's Mike Dillon said in the press the next day:

This five-timer did not hit us like a similar effort would on the flat by Frankie Dettori. Sadly, because of his injuries Adrian Maguire has lost his position in the affection of punters. A few years ago it would have been different. But now Tony McCoy is the darling boy of the thousands of betting-shop punters. He is way ahead in the pecking order with the betting-shop faithfuls. He has reached the Lester Piggott status, in that gamblers will back his rides without even looking at the form, or the trainer, of his horses. They only have to see A. P. McCoy in the newspaper and they want to get on. The McCoy factor is now something we have become very much aware of daily.

I have seen the way Richard Dunwoody has become so obsessed about riding winners, and although I have a similar thirst for winners, I hope that I can keep the whole business in perspective. I work hard, travel seventy thousand miles a year, and risk life and limb virtually every half an hour, every afternoon throughout the year. I feel very strongly that you have to get greedy while you have the chance. As we say back in Northern Ireland, 'It's not a bother, so it isn't.'

CHAPTER 1

'Wee Aunthnay'

Tony McCoy's father Peadar never sat on a horse in his life, yet he bred a succession of top jumpers . . . and the human tornado McCoy Jnr, who has taken English racing by storm in such a short space of time.

Anthony Peter, as he was christened, emerged from his parents' post office and village store in the tiny village of Moneyglass to be a riding sensation in England. Moneyglass is just a mile from the town of Toomebridge in County Antrim, right in the middle of one of Ulster's most fertile and prosperous farming regions. It is close to the vast Lough Neagh to the south, and on the banks of Northern Ireland's longest river, the River Bann, teeming with trout and salmon. Bomb-scarred Belfast, torn in two by centuries of religious strife, is only thirty-five miles away from the peace and quiet of friendly Moneyglass.

Toomebridge is well known as the home of legendary Ireland and British Lions rugby ace Willie John McBride, who was born less than a mile away from Tony McCoy's first home, and actor Richard Todd, famous for many film roles, including that of Guy Gibson in the 1954 film The Dambusters.

Tony McCoy is one of six children born to Peadar and Claire McCoy. His two older sisters are Anne-Marie, who works at the local County Hall, and hairdresser Roysin, who lives with her

*husband Diarmuid Shivers and their small baby in a cottage right
on the banks of the River Bann. Tony has two younger sisters,
Jayne and Kelly. His brother, Colm, is a former all-Ireland boxing
champion, fighting with the Errigal Amateur Boxing Club from
Garvagh. He won titles in the thirty-nine-kilos division.*

C.D.

I sat on a horse almost before I could walk. My father popped
me on our mare Misclaire, mother of the 1993 County Hurdle
winner Thumbs Up at the Cheltenham Festival, when I was just
two years old. It's one of my first memories back home in
Northern Ireland and I'm chuffed that somebody just happened
to take a photograph of A. P. McCoy's first ride.

As I grew up I was crazy about every sport – snooker, Gaelic
football, soccer, and any team games we could play round my
home near Toomebridge. From an early age I was allowed to
watch football on television, and at that stage my biggest ambition was to walk out at Highbury in the number nine shirt for
Arsenal. I was Arsenal crazy. There were a number of Irishmen in
their double-winning side and I was especially keen on Liam
Brady. I thought that he was a great player.

Another early memory is of my father taking me to the opening of
a sports shop in Magherafelt in County Derry by Arsenal goalkeeper
Pat Jennings. I took a football along and had it autographed by
Jennings; it was my most prized possession for years.

My father had lots of Catholic friends, who were great Celtic
supporters, and twice he took me over to Scotland to watch them.
That was great, and although I was very young I can remember
the tremendous atmosphere.

I was given a snooker cue for Christmas once and this sport
suddenly became my big love. I used to imagine that I was
Hurricane Higgins, although I was so tiny I could barely reach
to play my shots.

My father always bred a few horses in a field at the back of our bungalow, but I didn't take the slightest interest. Apart from him, nobody had horses for a five-mile radius about us.

I went to local point-to-points with my father, which I thought were quite exciting. I used to stand and watch the hectic action of the bookies and their tic-tac men. Still it never registered that this was the sport I should become involved in.

My first pony was mad. If she had been a human she would have been put into a straitjacket and locked up. She was absolutely crackers but she was the best-looking pony you ever saw in your life. She looked like a little Arabian mare, worth a million dollars. My father bought her as an unbroken three-year-old, to try and get me interested in ponies. She had ability and could jump six foot, but she had a hundred tricks to get me dumped off. She sometimes refused even to go near the posts and fences my father had put up in our field.

We got one of the stablelads from the nearby stables of professional trainer Billy Rock to try and sort her out. She looked a racy sort and this lad duly jumped on top. They were last seen running straight through a hedge. We eventually got her in foal and she moved on.

Father then got hold of my second pony, called Chippy – the first old rogue was never officially named, although I had plenty of names for her. Chippy was completely different. She was a very competitive little pony and could jump like a cat. She was also fast, and I began to appreciate the thrill of flying over obstacles, although I had lots of falls and was nearly buried about once a week. We won plenty of pony shows and gymkhanas around Magherafelt and Ballymena, and my bedroom was full of rosettes and trophies, but suddenly I found that it was too slow and not competitive enough – I got bored as hell just waiting around to go into the ring.

Chippy did give me the biggest fright of my early years, and sailing over Becher's Brook in the Grand National later was a doddle compared to an experience I had in one of our fields. The little mare took off with me and I knew that there was no way on earth I was going to stop her. I tried to put on the brakes but she charged straight at a massive, bushy hedge. She completely cleared the hedge, but I was left stranded on the top of it. I remember sitting on top of that hedge with thorns sticking into my backside, thinking that I must be quite mad.

On Saturdays I watched the racing from England on television with my father and mother. I thought that Lester Piggott and Steve Cauthen were brilliant, and used to try and imagine the thrill they must have had from winning tight finishes. I can't recall seeing much jump racing at that stage, and I can barely remember watching John Francome – dubbed 'The World's Greatest Jockey' by John McCririck – as he had retired before I became keen on the sport.

I used to run betting errands for my family. I was under age, but the local bookie always let one of the grown-ups actually place the wagers. I remember my late grandmother having five pounds on Last Suspect to win the 1985 Grand National. We all went raving mad when Hywel Davies won at 50–1. Within a few years I would be riding for Last Suspect's trainer, Tim Forster.

I had a very happy childhood. In a family of six children there were the inevitable fights and arguments, but I cannot praise my parents enough. They put up with a lot from me, but I never wanted for anything . . . apart from being forced to go to school.

I hated school, loathed every second I was there. I started at Toome Primary School and later went on to St Olcan's High School at Randalstown. The best part of school was the sport and PE and playing Gaelic football for my local club St Ergnat's. There was nothing wrong with any of the teachers, it was just that I was so bored with the lessons – especially French and music – and I simply wanted to be at home.

When I was nine years old I had a terrible experience. My father asked the girl who lived next door to drive me in her car to pick up some horsenuts from Toomebridge. When we reached the main crossroads in the middle of the town, another car came speeding straight at us. My head thumped against the side window and actually went through the glass, and I needed four stitches. Perhaps the bump made me see sense – it was horses and not school for me in the future.

By the time I was eleven years old I started to be sick every Monday and Tuesday. Then it was Wednesdays and the odd Friday. I came up with every excuse I could think of. In the end it became a major problem and I was simply breaking the law. My mother was in fierce trouble, and the schools' attendance officer was always hammering on the door.

Ducking school was suddenly the only thing in life I cared about. It wasn't that I was the school dunce – actually, I did quite well in some subjects. My father was a joiner, and I enjoyed the woodwork and metalcraft, but I hated everything else. Homework simply involved getting on the bus in the morning and scribbling anything down in a last-minute mad panic, or trying to persuade my friends to let me copy some answers.

My father was sympathetic. As I was so keen on the pony, and had some riding ability, he thought it was best to let me do my own thing. Mother, however, was furious about me not going to school. She is very strong willed, but I am as well, so it led to some terrible fights. Most mornings I would punch and swing my arms to avoid going to school. I even tried throwing my school satchel away to get out of catching the school bus. My father would say, 'It's not a bother, Anthony is not going to school,' but it was Mother who had to answer the door when teachers came round looking for me.

Every Saturday morning my father used to drive the ten miles or so to Billy Rock's racehorse stables to look at his yard. I started to go with him, and one day they put me up on the former Maktoum horse Wood Louse and let me walk him round the roads. Then I started to canter him. After riding Chippy, this was a different game altogether and I was hooked. I'm afraid that after riding a proper racehorse I never went near my pony again. I never even bothered to go into her field to say goodbye. My life had moved on and my only ambition was to spend as much time as I could manage in Billy Rock's stables with his horses.

*   *   *

Tony's mother remembers: 'One October time he started at Billy Rock's stables, and he never went back to school at all. It was so embarrassing as the teachers from St Olcan's High School, Randalstown, were ringing up to enquire where Tony was. I made hundreds of excuses from sore throats to chicken pox. Then it got worse and they would come round knocking on the front door. I used to make more excuses and say he was very unwell. But all the time I was hoping and praying that he would not come flying round the corner on his bicycle after a day's work with the horses at Billy Rock's stables.

'In the end we had to accept that his schooling was never going to work. One day, before he got his bike, I insisted on him going to school and refused to take him in the car to Billy Rock's place. But he just put his foot down and threatened to ring for a taxi if I would not take him. I am sure that in their hearts the teachers knew that he was obviously going to do something in his life with horses and they turned a blind eye to him playing truant. I fought some right battles with Anthony to try and get him to school. We argued and he cried, but he won.

'One evening we were called to a parents' meeting and I took Anthony along. He was really into the stable work by then and his school report was mostly empty – blank spaces. The principal asked Anthony what he wanted to be when he left school and he mumbled, "I'm going to be a jockey." The principal never heard him correctly and thought that he said a joiner, like his father.'

After Tony had won his second jump jockeys' title in 1997, Billy Rock recalled, 'I had been friends with Anthony's father Peadar for over twenty years. Most Saturdays Peadar would come up to the stables to see my horses work. One week he walked into the stables and introduced me to wee Anthony – he was just twelve years old and very small.

'I agreed to employ him on Saturdays, but that soon became

weekends. In no time at all he was virtually working full-time. I let him ride two of my racehorses round the all-weather gallop and the kid was hooked. I don't know what he had. It was some kind of uncanny gift. Within weeks he was riding racehorses which it took two full-grown men to hold either side. Often some of my staff would jump off these big old chasers and say, "Sod that, I'm not riding that beast again!" But Anthony seemed to be able to calm down the most dangerous of horses.

'He'd only had a handful of riding lessons but even at that age he could get on the biggest of my horses and ride them round a field on a slack rein. If I had not seen it with my own eyes, I would never have believed it. Nobody taught McCoy. Anything he picked up was completely self taught. If he did have the odd fall when schooling horses he was always very manly. There were never any tears.

'Anthony always had tremendous courage and nothing seemed to frighten him even though he was still tiny. He was the most reliable fella ever to walk into my yard. He had a one-track mind. He was almost blinkered himself and all he wanted to do was to work with horses. At fourteen he had a very old head on young shoulders and looked every inch a professional. He was a credit to his parents and now everybody in Northern Ireland is so proud that he has put this area firmly on the racing map. For a wee chap he would always ride very short and I used to joke with him that he must have been watching Lester Piggott on television. But at that time his idol was another lad from Northern Ireland – Richard Dunwoody.

'There was never any devilment in Anthony. He was very quiet and it was a job to get two words out of him. I watch him being interviewed now on television and can hardly believe it was the same lad sitting in my kitchen munching away at his Kit-Kat. On the gallops it was a miracle watching him in action. It was unbelievable to see the way for such a young buck he could see a stride in a horse at a fence. He was so polite all the time and a model stableman. I tell all my friends that there was never a curse on him . . . if he had not become champion jump jockey in

England he could have been a parish priest!'

* * *

I never went back to school, and left when I was fourteen. My O-level achievements are nil. Mother always said that I should have qualifications to fall back on, but I was suddenly so keen to be a jockey that I didn't care.

I did go back to St Olcan's High School, Randalstown once . . . as champion jockey elect to present their annual sports prizes in February 1996.

* * *

Robert Fenton wrote in the *Belfast Telegraph*:

Rising racing star Tony McCoy went back to school this week. Not to have any lessons – the twenty-one-year-old Moneyglass lad needs few of those. Tony was delighted to be the guest speaker, and it wasn't bad going considering that he was riding in the five thirty at Taunton that day and was back for the first race at Sandown the next day, where a double saw him increase his tally of winners to 112. His tip to the boys and girls was 'Stick with St Olcan's and you're sure to be on a winner.' Somewhat ironic considering that Tony often 'mitched' school to develop his riding talent with Cullybackey trainer Billy Rock. Tony left school early at fourteen, but that betrays a bright, affable and articulate young man with his feet firmly on the ground.

* * *

Everybody at the school made me very welcome that night. It is a good school, although I can honestly say that the only time I ever enjoyed walking through the school gates was at that sports prize-giving as an old boy. Despite going on to become champion jockey, I'm afraid I'm not a good advertisement for education.

Nowadays, my riding exploits in England are the talk of the local town. My mother, whose bubbling, extrovert personality is in sharp contrast to my shy, quiet-spoken father is often stopped.

Shoppers and betting-shop regulars all have the same question for her when she walks down the main high street of Toomebridge: 'Anything to back of Anthony's today?'

My mother Claire admits that some Saturday nights or Sunday mornings she really dreads going to mass at our local church. All her friends take an interest in my career and are always after tips. If I have a bad day and no winners, she knows that she'll get a nudge at mass and people will ask, 'What went wrong today, why didn't he have any winners?' It's the same when my father goes to his local pub: everybody wants to know what Anthony fancies. Mother's friends think she knows so much about it, they call her John McCririck. My parents have SIS (Satellite Information Services) installed in their house, and watch nearly all my races. Mother hates it when I have falls, and says it's always a great relief when she sees me down to ride in the next race.

*   *   *

Claire adds, 'Anthony has really put Toomebridge on the map. The local pubs go mad on a Saturday afternoon when they see him riding a winner on television. A lot of people in the area take an interest in racing purely because of Anthony.'

Looking back to those days of school truancy, she continues, 'By now trainer Billy Rock was the most important person in his life. I know that Billy was always going on about "Wee Aunthnay". He was always on about our son and I think it drove some of the other stablelads mad. But Anthony can be very stubborn and from those early days there was not the slightest doubt that one day he'd be a jockey.'

CHAPTER 2

'Who is that kid trying to impersonate Lester Piggott?'

Billy Rock, the jovial, ruddy-faced Cullybackey trainer from County Antrim, was the shamrock Svengali in Tony McCoy's formative years. From the moment in 1987 when 'wee Aunthnay' walked into the dual trainer's yard, Tony was hooked on racing. Rock recalls, 'From the time he was twelve years old he was riding as many as fourteen horses of mine a day, about half my stable. Even at that age I was paying him £100 a week in readies as he could do the work of three full-grown men.'

Rock took out his licence in 1975, and like most trainers in Ireland, has always been a wheeler-dealer with horses. He loves recounting the occasion when Nicky Henderson, one of England's top jump trainers, visited his Cullybackey stables on a typical horse-scouting mission. The Old Etonian, who was champion trainer in England in 1985–6 and 1986–7, largely due to Champion Hurdler See You Then, always took in Rock's stables to run his eyes over the young bumper and point-to-point horses.

With a healthy chuckle Rock says, 'I asked Anthony to canter a horse, who was for sale, round one of our fields. I'll never forget Henderson leaning against a post-and-rail fence and saying with a smirk, "Who is that kid trying to impersonate Lester Piggott?"'

'People say that I was smart to spot Anthony's talents, but it was the easiest thing in the world. It was like a football talent scout in the back streets of Belfast spotting George Best. Anthony

*had that special gift. He had ability and style and the guts to go
with it.'*

*It was Rock, who trained Eddy Wee to be fifth in the 1981
Waterford Supreme Novices' Hurdle under amateur Ted Walsh at
the Cheltenham Festival, who fashioned raw McCoy's talents into
the champion jockey he is today.*

C.D.

I got the racing bug from a horse called Wood Louse, the first
horse I was allowed to ride for Billy Rock. He had broken his
knee and was an ideal quiet horse to learn on. He was owned by
the Maktoums and had one race on the flat for Curragh trainer
John Oxx before he suffered his injury. After one canter on him at
Billy Rock's Cullybackey stables I was hooked, and my poor old
pony Chippy had to go. Wood Louse may have broken his knee,
but he soon recovered, and the thrill of cantering him at speed was
quite amazing.

Eddy Wee was another horse I loved riding. He was the pride of
the stables after running such a big race under Ted Walsh at the
1981 Cheltenham Festival, and he went on to win the big two-mile
races at Punchestown and Fairyhouse.

One day I was walking Eddy Wee at exercise on the lonely roads
around Cullybackey, where traffic was almost non-existent. A
woman in a car came round the corner and kindly slowed right
down. However, as she drew level with Eddy Wee and myself, she
suddenly put her foot on the accelerator and the engine made a loud
noise. Eddy Wee tried to jump on top of the car and gave it a terrible
kicking. I was sure the driver would get out and there would be a
dreadful row, but she must have realised that she was in the wrong.
She slowly drove off with huge dents all down the side of her car,
and, uninjured, Eddy Wee and I carried on with our walk.

Billy Rock seemed to take a liking to me, and some of the older
lads were not over the moon about it. One day they told me to ride

Eddy Wee in a covered barn area. I knew he was fresh and would try and buck me off – he was an expert at bucking his riders off. I wasn't wrong, and crashed to the sand floor, much to the amusement of the other lads. Still, they were happy days and I couldn't get there quick enough every morning to help with all the grubby jobs.

Billy Rock is a rather arrogant man, and would be the first one to admit it. He is very intelligent and has bags of confidence in himself and the way he trains horses. However, I cannot speak too highly of him. He was very helpful to me and went out of his way to make sure that I was going to get on. At fourteen he was paying me a hundred pounds a week – the same as the older lads.

Although we were so close to Belfast, we never experienced any of the troubles. Indeed, apart from one or two shopping trips, one Christmas pantomime and the odd TV chat show appearance much later, I never went to Belfast. My family are all Catholics, but many of my father's point-to-point friends were Protestants, and religion never came into it. Billy Rock is also a Protestant. Rather than take sides about religion we often used to make light of it and have the odd joke. My mother would joke with Billy Rock that he wasn't going to the races because he was going to the Rev. Ian Paisley's Ballymena stronghold. Billy Rock would have a chuckle and reply, 'I suppose you are out tonight throwing stones at the soldiers!' It was all said in very good humour. Billy Rock was such a shrewd businessman that it didn't matter what religion you were. You could be white, black or purple if you were signing a cheque to buy one of his horses.

Billy is very much involved in his other business of the artificial insemination of cows. He would often go off for the day and leave me in charge of all the gallops and feeding, even though there was no way that the other lads – some as old as twenty-four and twenty-five – were going to take orders from a little fourteen-year-old fella like me.

I loved the life with Billy Rock, especially riding the horses in fast work, and leading up horses at the races. I often used to go in the horse lorry to tracks in the north, like Down Royal and

Downpatrick. Sometimes I'd travel with Billy Rock in his car to the races, something that drove all the other lads mad with envy as they squeezed into the horse lorry. They probably thought that I would sneak on them and tell tales to the guv'nor, but I never did.

Looking back it's obvious that I was actually breaking the law as I should have been at school. However, my mother, who was by then running the family store and post office behind our house, had realised that I was a definite 'non-runner' at school.

I loved to get to the yard before the trainer. I cycled in all weathers, which was made easier when I bought myself a racing bicycle, and mucked out many horses a day, something I'd find too much like hard work these days.

Conor O'Dwyer, who was a seven-pound claimer in those days, used to ride a lot of work and in races for Billy Rock, and I loved watching him ride. He rode much shorter than all the other Irish jump jockeys and was always very brave. I took part in many schooling sessions at Dundalk racecourse after racing, with experienced riders like Tony Powell and the amateur Anthony Martin. I was still only fourteen and technically you are not allowed to ride on a racecourse until you are sixteen, but that did not worry Billy Rock. He was very shrewd when it came to getting his way. He would have kept a straight face while telling lies to the Pope if he thought he'd get away with it. He never really had a care in the world, and used the same Northern Ireland expression as my father – 'not a bother'.

I was beginning to adopt my own style of riding, although I never really had any lessons. I tried to put just my toe in the iron, like flat jockeys, and not sit upright like some jump riders, who look more like policemen on horseback. I suppose I was trying to perfect the toe-in-the-iron style used by modern-day flat champions Frankie Dettori and Michael Kinane. I wasn't vain, but I was terribly interested in how I looked on horseback. I'd use any method of looking at myself. I remember looking at shadows to see if I was riding in the correct position, and loved passing big windows as it gave me a chance to see myself. I even looked at cars parked by the stables to see my reflection.

In those days I was so small it was unbelievable – a five-stone titch, barely five feet tall. Back then the last thing I ever imagined in the world was that I would shoot up to nearly six foot, and that by far the biggest struggle in my life would be to tip the scales at ten stone, with all the terrible fasting and sweating which it now involves.

Billy Rock was so convinced that I'd make it as a flat jockey that he contacted Jim Bolger, the well-known trainer from County Carlow.

*   *   *

Billy recalls, 'By the summer of 1989 I realised that Anthony had such great talent that he needed a job with a bigger stable. I had done quite a bit of business with Jim Bolger from Coolcullen in the south in County Carlow, so I rang him one day and said, "I have a future champion flat jockey for you." In those days I never dreamed that Anthony would switch full-time to jumping as he was still so minute.

'Jim Bolger replied, "Champion jockey – that's quite a statement."

'He agreed to take Anthony and so his career moved on another stage. I knew that Jim Bolger was a hard man to please and he had the reputation for being a firm taskmaster. He didn't suffer fools at all – let alone easily – but I knew that he would knock the rough edges off Anthony and turn him into a fine flat rider.'

*   *   *

It was agreed that I should spend two weeks with Jim Bolger on a trial. It was only the second time that I had been across the border and deep into the south. The previous occasion was when I was taken as a wee lad to see the Irish Grand National at Fairyhouse by my father.

Staying with Jim Bolger for two weeks was a great experience, although I have to admit that as a naive fifteen-year-old who had never left home, at first I was actually frightened of this seemingly hard, cold man. He was a tough taskmaster and made it very clear that his word was law. I remember arriving at the Glebe House stables in Coolcullen. To be fair, Jim Bolger made me very welcome but after my parents had left for the four-hour drive back to the north, I found myself wondering what the hell I was doing there. The other lads in the digs were very pleasant, however, and it was not long before we all trooped off to a local pub to play pool.

Christy Roche was then the top jockey at Jim Bolger's, and I naturally found it fascinating to see him riding potential Classic horses. Paul Carberry was also there as a youngster. I decided after those two weeks that I wanted to be a flat jockey, and happily signed the apprenticeship forms which Jim Bolger offered.

Sadly, I never actually rode in a race for Billy when I was at his stables. I had hoped to win for him on his Della Wee at Perth on the opening day of the 1995–96 season, but sadly the horse bolted going to the start and that was virtually it. We were up with the leaders but weakened after three hurdles and finished sixth. I was also unplaced on Billy Rock's Clever Folly in the next race, a handicap chase. I managed to get off the mark when the John White-trained Googly won the novices' chase by seven lengths. She started 6–4 favourite and overcame a mistake at the last fence to win. The next day at Perth, 9 June, I was so pleased to score for Billy Rock on his game Tabu Lady in the novices' hurdle. She proved a tough little character, and zoomed away to a five-length victory after taking the lead two flights from home. As I said at the time, that was the one I wanted.

*   *   *

Billy says of that win at Perth, 'Anthony was especially thrilled at having his first win for us. Actually he had to work so hard on her that when he got off I thought he was going to be physically sick. He even told me that he would probably not be able to ride in the next race. But, of course, he did and duly won on Secretary of State for Lambourn trainer David Arbuthnot, by eleven lengths.'

*   *   *

The follow-up to Nicky Henderson's visit to Northern Ireland and his question of 'Who is that kid trying to impersonate Lester Piggott?' is that he has in later years tried to book me on many occasions. However, it always seems to be when I am already fixed for another ride. In fact, the Lambourn trainer who spotted me all those years ago on Billy Rock's gallops has only used me once – I rode his Golden Spinner to win the Badger Novices' Chase at Sandown on 6 February 1996.

CHAPTER 3

'Jim Bolger could train a goat to win a race'

Tony McCoy's schooling in racing came at trainer Jim Bolger's remarkable academy at Coolcullen, a mountaintop, blue-chip training centre in County Carlow, some thousand feet above sea level. Billy Rock's huge point-to-pointers in Northern Ireland were a far cry from shrewd Jim Bolger's bluebloods in the south.

Jim Bolger was born on Christmas Day in 1941 and many of his bold Classic triumphs suggest that he can even walk on water. As Tony O'Hehir reported in the Racing Post: 'This birthday has encouraged those who consider him a rather self-righteous individual to make obvious comparisons.'

Wexford-born Bolger, a former accountant in the offices of a Dublin car dealer, is a no-nonsense loner, who has hit the Classic jackpot with 1992 Irish Derby winner St Jovite and the 1991 50–1 Epsom Oaks heroine Jet Ski Lady. He does not court friendship with his equals and does not conform to the usual perception of an Irish trainer. The only bar you are likely to spot Bolger attending is in a court of law, such as when he successfully appealed for a fifteen-day ban for his jockey Christy Roche to be delayed until after the Irish Derby, which he then won with St Jovite.

Bolger, who admits that he solved his acute financial problems back in April 1962 by having a pound each way on the Grand National winner Kilmore at 33–1, is uncompromising. He was the tutor who really fashioned Tony McCoy's career at the most *important stage of his life. Tony readily admits, 'Without Jim Bolger, I would not be where I am today.'*

Jimmy Walker of the Belfast Telegraph *says, 'The old image of Irish trainers going around with hay coming out of their ears went out in the thirties. Now men like Jim Bolger, Dermot Weld and John Oxx are international trainers and millionaires. I remember one day Jim Bolger had a winner at Leopardstown, and I commented that the horse was a front-runner. Bolger said, "All my horses are front-runners . . . I'm a front-runner myself." There is no doubt that Jim holds himself in great esteem, but his record proves that he is an outstanding trainer.*

'I like the story of the occasion when Jim Bolger had an open day at his stables and one of his old schoolmates went along. He approached Jim and said, "Hello, you won't remember me but I was in your class at school."

'Bolger grinned: "I'm in a different class now."'

When Bolger told me, 'I shall win the Irish Derby again,' I did not doubt him for one moment. He is fiercely ambitious and it is his totally blinkered yearning for success which has rubbed off on Tony McCoy and made him the most successful graduate of Jim Bolger's remarkable racing academy.

C.D.

The biggest turning point of my life came when I travelled with my parents to Dundalk races on 13 July 1989, the day I signed a three-year apprenticeship to join Jim Bolger in Coolcullen, County Carlow. I actually went to the races to lead up a couple of runners for Billy Rock, but the important moment came when I had to sign the forms. Jim Bolger was not at Dundalk that day and the papers were signed by myself, my parents, and Jim's then travelling head lad Tom Gallagher, father of fellow jump jockey Dean, who has since become travelling head lad to Dermot Weld on the Curragh.

On the way to the races my mother was very anxious. She was not so sure that signing my life away for three years was such a good idea. I could see that she was very worried, and I tried to reassure her by saying, 'I would like to be a brain surgeon – but I don't have the brains.' She was always frightened that I would not make a go of it as an apprentice jockey, and given my lack of school attendance, I would have no other career to fall back on. In contrast my father always went along with the idea. He knew that my heart was set on a career with horses, although at that stage I saw myself as a future flat jockey and had no thought that one day I'd switch to jumping.

This was it, however, and my parents knew it. I was to be gone for three years, and it would be the end of my life at home. My mother kept asking me if I was sure I wanted to do this. The rules in Ireland were strict, and if you signed with a trainer for three years, you had to complete those three years with him before you could ride for anyone else, unless he decided to release you from the contract.

I journeyed down to Jim Bolger's place in the mountains in his horsebox and moved into digs with Mrs Murphy in a house at the bottom of the hill from Jim Bolger's stables. I arrived with just one suitcase, and apart from trips back when I broke my leg and with other lesser injuries, I have seldom been home to Northern Ireland.

My first week's wages were ninety pounds, so I actually took a wage cut to join one of Ireland's most famous trainers. With working at weekends, I had managed to pick up a hundred pounds a week from Billy Rock, when I was supposed to be still a schoolboy. We were in the yard by seven o'clock and worked until one o'clock. Then we would be off until two fifteen when we worked through to five thirty.

I loved the new life with Jim Bolger, but I was also terribly homesick for the first few months. My mother phoned two or three times a week and I tried to put on a brave act, although there were plenty of other young lads in the same situation. We had all left the comfort of our homes and were trying to make a go of it in racing. All the lads used to gather at the local Maloney's pub, but I never touched a drop of alcohol and haven't done so to this day.

I did miss home, but the digs were friendly and were also used by Jim Bolger's head lad Pat O'Donavan and the jockey Willie Supple. Paul Carberry, later to join me in England as a jump jockey, was also there at the time, but my special pal was Conor Everard, who came from Tipperary. He had the magic advantage of having a car and gave me lifts to the local sauna and swimming-pool. He was a real friend and never left me stuck for a lift back to our digs. If we went into the local big town of Carlow, which was about twenty minutes away, he always made sure that he never left me behind. Another youngster who was to make it as a flat jockey later was Seamus Heffernan.

Jim Bolger was a hard man to work for. It was not easy for a raw youngster, but if any of his staff wanted help he would be the first to give assistance. If any of the lads got into trouble he would also be the first to step in with a helping hand.

Looking back, we were all scared stiff of Jim Bolger, and the message would soon go round the yard when he was walking down from the big house. If anybody was skiving, they soon jumped to.

He was tough on us lads but he was also very fair. There is no way that I would be where I am today if it was not for Jim Bolger, something I can state without any hesitation, even though we were to cross swords later when I wanted to come to England. Okay, he could be very sharp with the lads, but he had to knock us into line. It was impossible to win an argument with him. He would never argue with his staff, unless he knew that he was in the right.

We all feared Bolger, but there was another side to him. He could also be incredibly generous. My first Christmas at the stable he handed me a £500 bonus before my sister collected me for five days' leave. He was like that and it made up for all the hard work. We were rather cut off at the stables, but Bolger arranged trips to Dublin for shows and the theatre. He was also keen on Gaelic football and hurling, and encouraged us to go to matches.

The gallops used to echo with his shouts. He knew what he wanted from us youngsters, and was determined to drill it into us. Jim Bolger was very keen on the riding style of his lads from the very first day they arrived, and was very firm that we should ride with our toes in the iron and adopt the straight-back style of Michael Kinane and Steve Cauthen. He was adamant about this, and loved to see the American style of riding.

* * *

Jim Bolger says, 'I have a policy with my apprentices and I drum into them that it does not matter whether they win or lose, as long as they look good. I wouldn't want that theory to be too rigid but my basic message to all young jockeys is to be neat and tidy and the rest will come. I was very keen to see my riders put just their toe in the iron. The Americans are far smarter than us in this respect. Riders can get dragged if they get hung up in the irons. We all remember Lester Piggott getting hung into the irons when Durtal misbehaved before the 1977 Oaks at Epsom and I did not want to see that ever happen again. Durtal was favourite and never even took part in the Oaks.'

* * *

The first horse I looked after was the mare Easy To Please, who had won the Queen Alexandra Stakes at Royal Ascot in 1991 under our top stable jockey at the time, Christy Roche. It was a terrific training performance as it was her first outing of the season as a four-year-old. I can remember all the stablelads watching on TV in Jim Bolger's staff canteen and cheering like mad when Christy shot to the front a furlong out and went on to beat Pat Eddery on the 2–1 favourite Nomadic Way by seven lengths. We were not allowed to bet, of course, but I do know that Easy To Please was at 8–1 that day.

I started the apprenticeship in July but it was a year and a half before I rode proper work. However, it was good experience as I rode out as many as six or seven lots of work a day on very different horses. Christy Roche, Willie Supple and Conor O'Dwyer rode all the main work on the stable's top horses, while Paul Carberry, Seamus Heffernan and myself had to wait our turn. Jim Bolger came down for every lot. He seemed to walk everywhere, and I never saw him watching the gallops in a car like some trainers. I only saw him actually ride out a few times, when he partnered Paul Green's Elementary, a horse who was later to join Martin Pipe in England.

Jim Bolger is like Martin Pipe, in that they had little experience in racing when they started and made their own way to the top. Neither would suffer fools easily. The Boss was very strict on smoking and drinking. If any lad was caught in the main yard with a trace of smoke on his breath, he was sacked! No questions. Lads might have a quick drag in Carlow, some twenty minutes' drive away, but they knew better than to be caught smoking anywhere near the horses.

He was equally anti-drinking. Raymond Smith's book *Tigers of the Turf* relates how the author confessed that he liked nothing better than to have a few drinks before dinner and share a bottle of wine over the meal itself. Bolger said, 'You can count yourself lucky if you can control matters in that way. Not everyone is so lucky. So few can drink in moderation that I maintain that it's an almost impossible situation to achieve. People think that they are letting their hair down and then go too far and the consequences can be terribly serious, especially if someone is involved in an accident after taking too much drink. The wisest course to pursue is to stay clear of it altogether.'

Religion played a big part in Jim Bolger's life and he insisted that we all took part. All through Lent, every morning the entire stable staff would be ordered to attend mass at the local church. The priest had to organise the service to fit in with the time of our morning gallops. After first lot, thirty or forty of us, still wearing our riding gear and breeches, filed into the church for mass.

Some lads could not stand Bolger's strict regime. Some came from homes miles away in Ireland, like me, but could not take the harsh change. Some lasted a few months, others did a runner after just a couple of days. But I realised that I was lucky to be part of such a fabulous set-up and was determined to stick it out.

I was lucky that Billy Rock tipped off Jim Bolger about me. It was a hard but perfect introduction into a major stable. To this day it is as good a set-up as I have ever seen and I've been in countless stables now to ride work. The gallop is quite fantastic, and is the best all-weather surface I have ever ridden on. It starts with a gradual incline and then rises sharply. It has two turns on the way but the horses hardly notice it. The Boss is so shrewd that before he made his successful raids on Epsom he used to work the horses down the wrong way of the gallop to get them used to the downhill parts with turns.

One of Jim Bolger's assistants at this time was Aidan O'Brien, who was later to shatter all Irish jump records, and a few flat ones on the way as well. In 1994 he smashed Dermot Weld's record of 150 winners in a year. He shares the same surname as the great Vincent O'Brien but is no relation. Aidan he left Jim Bolger to set up on his own, and was later to use Vincent's world-famous Ballydoyle gallops. He had ridden his first winner as an amateur jockey for Jim Bolger on Galacto Boy at Punchestown on 11 January 1989, and became champion amateur rider in Ireland in 1993–4. He had his first winner as a trainer, Wandering Thoughts, at Tralee on 7 June 1993. His first Cheltenham Festival winner came when Urubande won the 1996 Sun Alliance Novices' Hurdle, when I was fourth on David Nicholson's Jack Tanner. In 1997 Aidan won the Supreme Novices' Hurdle with Istabraq, who may well be challenging Make A Stand for the 1998 Champion Hurdle.

My memory of Aidan in those days at Jim Bolger's is that he was a lot heavier – he has lost weight since he switched to training. Aidan did not have a great deal of experience with horses when he joined Jim Bolger, but was yet another graduate from the Coolcullen academy to shine later. Jim Bolger was always very keen for Aidan to ride difficult horses as he seemed to have a natural flair for sorting out the troublemakers on the gallops.

In 1997 Aidan O'Brien won the first three Irish Classics with Desert King (2,000 Guineas), Classic Park (1,000 Guineas), and Desert King again (the Irish Derby). At the age of 27, Aidan has already become a legend.

I waited a long time to ride in real fast pieces of work, but then it was not long before Jim Bolger gave me a chance to ride in my first race. The sleepiest, quietest horse in his yard was called Nordic Torch. Actually he was a little fella, often as fat as a barrel. He was a complete piss-taker as a horse and never did his best. He did not do a stroke on the gallops at home and never won a race before or after I rode him. Phoenix Park on 1 September 1990 was the venue for my first public appearance.

Nordic Torch had been second in big fields and had run well at Leopardstown for Richard Hughes, when carrying just seven stone. At Phoenix Park he carried 6st 11lb and I tipped the scales at 6st 4lb. I was thrilled that my father came down from the north of Ireland to watch the race. Billy Rock was also there to see my first ride in public. I walked the course with Jim Bolger before the six-furlong race and he told me exactly where he wanted me to be. Christy Roche was on a fancied horse for Curragh trainer Mick O'Toole and my strict orders were to track him throughout the race. I can remember the stalls opening but I never saw Christy! The race was over in a flash, and it was a far cry from the long-distance races like the Scottish Grand National, which I was later to win. To this day I don't know a lot about my first ride, except that I was a 6st 4lb flyweight and as weak as a kitten. Still, Jim Bolger was quite pleased afterwards with my display with unplaced Nordic Torch, who carried his wife Jackie's colours of white with a purple line.

My second ride came as a spare ride when I rode Nordic Wind at the Curragh and was second. I was beaten by another of Jim Bolger's horses, who was ridden by Willie Supple. I had no idea that I was going to get this ride, but Christy Roche could not make the weight.

My first-ever flat winner came on 20–1 Legal Steps in the Silvermines Maiden at Thurles on 20 March, 1992. The filly was by Law Society, and again Jim Bolger had two in the race, with Christy Roche on a more fancied runner. My filly was unfancied and untipped at 20–1. The Boss was not at the races but told me before I left for Thurles that I might have a bit of a chance. He believed all his horses had a chance, and they were certainly always out to do their best. Like Martin Pipe, he craved winners too much ever to dream of a non-trier.

Horses at Coolcullen were never set up for gambles, and Jim Bolger was always happy to tell you the name of horses you were trying out on the gallops. There was no cloak and dagger stuff and he never messed about with the weights.

I won the one-and-a-half-mile maiden quite easily. It was unbelievable. She just kept going and I knew a long way out that I was not going to be headed. The Boss always obtained videos of races when he was not present, and next day he greeted me with a smile and simply said, 'Well done.' No matter how many races I win, I'll never forget the first time I came back to the winners' enclosure.

I loved riding my first winner but it was back to work the next day riding several lots on the gallops. My parents were over the moon, though, and one of the happiest telephone calls I ever received was when I got back to my digs and they rang to say that they were thrilled.

Many might think that Christy Roche would be annoyed that a stable claiming jockey had beaten him in a race, but that was far from the truth, and Christy was the first to offer his congratulations. Although Christy was champion jockey of the country, he was very helpful to me and I picked up tips galore from him. Like Jim Bolger, he is very smart. They don't come any sharper than this pair. Christy was very switched on – sometimes too switched on for his own good. However, he never begrudged me my first winner. He knew racing inside out and it was no surprise to those of us who knew him when he made such an immediately successful start to training.

My next winner came the following year when Galladini won at Leopardstown in one of the heats of the Derrestown Stud Apprentice series competition. He was a short-priced favourite but the rules of the competition were that the apprentice jockeys were not allowed to carry whips. I thought that I done a good job when I won, but as I dismounted I heard Jim Bolger tell his head lad Pat O'Donavan, 'McCoy has got a bit too cocky for his own good.' I suppose that I may have been a bit over-confident, but I was always sure that I was going to win.

If joining Jim Bolger was the most significant move of my career at that time, the next big event happened one cold, snowy January morning in 1993 on the Coolcullen all-weather gallop. I was riding a lovely Maktoum Green Desert colt called Kly Green. He was a yearling coming up as a two-year-old, and although he was an absolute picture to look at, I realised that he had a bit of a fiery temper. This particular morning he was bucking quite a bit on the gallops. He stumbled and I came off. It was an easy fall but I came crashing down on my left leg. I knew immediately that I had broken my leg. I can still remember the terrible pain from the fall and the icy-cold weather gnawing at my bones as I lay dumped in the snow.

Jim Bolger was soon on the scene, and I will always remember his words to me as I lay moaning and groaning on the ground: 'You're soft.'

Soft or not, I knew that my leg had been broken, and because of the snow on the gallops it took some forty-five minutes before an ambulance could make its way up the side of the hill to where I was lying. I was lucky that the very best surgeon in Kilkenny hospital was on hand to look after me, and I was in plaster from my toes to the top of my left leg.

Despite this crashing fall I was determined not to pack up, and still dreamed of being the next Christy Roche. However, that fall from Kly Green was to change my entire career and lead to my ultimate bust-up with the Boss.

I was in hospital for a few days before being driven back to my parents' home in County Antrim. It seems that the only time I make a pilgrimage back to Toomebridge is when I have suffered a bad fall. When the plaster eventually came off I was able to ride out on a quiet horse belonging to my father. In all, I had five months away from Jim Bolger's stables to recover fully.

My mother has always been a first-class cook. My sisters may prefer the trendy pasta dishes, but my mother knows that I love chops and juicy steaks. I am in a career where the bathroom scales are as important to me as a front-door key, but I make no bones about the fact that I love my grub. It breaks my heart to turn down food at dinner parties, but I know that I must be very careful. Being stuck at home for five months meant that I enjoyed one good feast after another, and it all added up. When I broke my leg I was a 7st 10lb beanpole; by the time I returned to County Carlow I had ballooned to 9st 7lb. I had put on the best part of two stone. In reality, it completely ended my flat career.

I did sweat like crazy to get back down to 7st 12lb to ride at Gowran Park afterwards, but all my strength had been sapped out of me. I tried getting the weight down but it was becoming an impossible task. It's been a constant struggle ever since, but I knew then in my heart that my flat jockey aspirations were a goner, and that I would have to concentrate on being a jump jockey. My flat career was not completely over, however, and I did ride another winner on Galladini, who also ran in Jim Bolger's wife's colours.

One bonus of my spending time with my parents in Toome-bridge was that I passed my driving test. Actually, I had been driving a little bit but had not actually got round to taking the test, which I then passed first time. With my savings and some help from my father, I bought a red Peugeot 205. It was my prize possession . . . but not for long! I had only had it a week and was driving south across the border back to Jim Bolger's stables when I took a corner too fast, lost control and wrote the car off. One of Jim Bolger's staff had to come and pick me up. After that my parents insisted that I got a Peugeot 205 van, as they thought that I was a lunatic on the road. When I moved to England, I brought the van over on the ferry and drove to Toby Balding's yard at Weyhill, Hampshire. But that ended in disaster as well. One day I was driving to Lingfield and was about five miles from Weyhill. I was a bit late and knew that I had to get a move on. I was going pretty fast round a corner, when I collided with a Range Rover and came off second best. My Peugeot van was another write-off, and again I had to ring my parents to tell them the sad news. My first two vehicles were like my first hurdle and chase rides in

Ireland – I failed to get round. My third car was a Volkswagen, and at least I did manage to keep this one on the highway. I never dreamed that one day I'd be presented with a £28,000 Saab for being champion jump jockey at the end of the 1996–7 season.

Many people in racing have a lot to thank the Maktoums for. The Arabs have piled literally billions of pounds into the sport and it's unthinkable what would happen if they suddenly pulled out of the game – there are a few Newmarket trainers who would be reaching for their shotguns. In a way, I suppose I must thank the Maktoum colt Kly Green for changing the whole outlook of my career – but for that fall on the gallops I could have remained focused on the flat game and never have made the switch to jumping.

Kly Green was second on his debut under Christy Roche at the Curragh in June 1993, behind Ben Hanbury's Polish Laughter, and then ended his two-year-old career by finishing seventh in the valuable Heinz 57 Stakes at Phoenix Park – a Group 1 race – in August 1993. The race was won by Robert Sangster's Turtle Island and the half-length runner-up was Tommy Stack-trained Las Meninas, who came out and won the 1,000 Guineas at Newmarket the next year. So I wasn't dumped by a complete no-hoper that cold January morning in the hills of County Carlow!

I now realised that my future lay in jump racing, although Jim Bolger was adamant that I still had a future as a flat jockey. He assured me that I would be able to ride all the top-weights from his stable in big handicaps and that there was a future for me on the level. When my three-year apprenticeship expired, I signed again, but only for a one-year period. After a lot of haggling it was agreed that I would promote my jumping career as a jockey, but I would stick to hurdles and never ride in chases.

These were exciting times at Coolcullen and Jim Bolger was really putting himself on the international stage. Back in 1981 he had first become known in England when his good filly Condessa hit the headlines. Early in the spring of that year she won a very moderate handicap at Clonmel, but Jim Bolger had sufficient faith to send her over for the Lingfield Oaks Trial, when she ran a blinder to be third behind Ian Balding's filly Leap Lively. Starting at 12–1, Condessa, who was ridden by Declan Gillespie, was only beaten by four lengths in this good trial, and fully justified Jim Bolger's raid to England.

If anybody thought that the Boss was aiming at the stars with Condessa, they found out soon. Returning to England for the Musidora Stakes at York – just four days later – Condessa started at 16–1 but floored a good field to win by four lengths, with the previous 1,000 Guineas winner Fairy Footsteps back in third. She then finished second to Blue Wind in the Irish Oaks at the Curragh in July, but returned to England for a third time and captured the Group 1 Yorkshire Oaks from Leap Lively by a neck, starting at 5–1. Jim Bolger had shown that he was a Group 1 trainer in Ireland and England. He built on his reputation as a great trainer of fillies, and after Condessa he saddled Park Appeal (Moyglare Stud Stakes and Cheveley Park Stakes in 1984), Park Express (1986 Phoenix Champion Stakes) and Polonia (1987 Prix de L'Abbaye at Longchamp).

In 1991 some folk thought that he was aiming too high again when he sent over Jet Ski Lady for the English Oaks at Epsom. She started at 50–1 and won the Oaks under Christy Roche. The Boss had been proved right again. I was lucky enough to ride Jet Ski Lady quite often at home. She was a really strong filly. I knew that she was decent but I must admit that I never thought of her as an Oaks winner. She never did anything really exciting at home, but Jim Bolger must have seen something to let her take her chance at Epsom. You could not argue with the trainer's record at Epsom, and in the 1993 Derby he saddled Blue Stag to be second behind Commander In Chief at 150–1.

The real star at Coolcullen during my time was without question St Jovite, who finished second in the Epsom Derby to Dr Devious in 1992, and then went on to gain his revenge by winning the Irish Derby and the Queen Elizabeth Diamond Stakes at Ascot in brilliant fashion. Aidan O'Brien always used to ride St Jovite in the early stages of the colt's two-year-old career. It was around this time that I first realised the genius that was ticking away in Jim Bolger's brain. St Jovite worked awfully as a two-year-old, and we had a dozen youngsters you would have picked in front of him, but I recall Jim Bolger saying, 'St Jovite is a Derby horse.' All the lads thought that he was mad. St Jovite was fourth in the Gladness Stakes as a three-year-old, and his work at home seemed to get slower and slower. To be honest, he was diabolical. The Boss worked him with slower horses, really moderate ones, to make him used to going by rivals on the gallops. The trick worked a treat and, although looking at one stage like he might be a potential hurdler, he turned into a top-class Classic winner. Jim Bolger had faith in him and saw something which escaped the rest of us. It showed what a super trainer I was lucky enough to be working with.

I rode in my first hurdle race at Leopardstown on 17 March 1994. I was a seven-pound claimer and pretty nervous. It was the very same day that Jodami and Mark Dwyer won the Cheltenham Gold Cup. I rode Riszard in a novice hurdle. Riszard was a good performer on the flat for the stable and in 1993 he won the Queen Alexandra Stakes at Royal Ascot, when Christy Roche got him up in the very last stride to pip Nigel Day on Jack Button by a short head. My first ride in a hurdle race did not end in a fairytale win, as I was brought down at the last hurdle. I got no bouquets from Jim Bolger, who informed me with one of his glares, 'You really are a greenhorn! You should have won.' I guess that he was not too annoyed with me, however, as he put me up on Riszard the next time he ran.

And the unknown winner of the first hurdle race I ever rode in? His name was Imperial Call, who was ridden to victory that day by Gerry O'Neill. He went on to win the 1996 Cheltenham Gold Cup, under Conor O'Dwyer, for that remarkable English trainer Fergie Sutherland, now based in County Cork, sparking off some of the happiest and wildest scenes ever in the Festival winners' enclosure. So just two years after riding in my first-ever hurdle race, I was having my second Cheltenham Gold Cup ride, on fourth-placed Barton Bank for David Nicholson, and seeing the same horse, Imperial Call, stride up the hill to a fantastic win.

The first time I ever sat on horseback. My father puts me up on our family mare Misclaire. My style doesn't look too bad for a two-year-old!

My first visit to a winners' enclosure . . . yes, I'm the young stable lad leading in Wood Louse after victory at Downpatrick. The jockey is Conor O'Dwyer and the happy lady on the left is Yvonne Rock, wife of trainer Billy Rock.

Riding a horse in a race for the first time. This is me on Nordic Torch at Phoenix Park on 1 September, 1990. I can't believe that I once tipped the scales at 6st. 4lb.

First race inquest . . . trainer Jim Bolger quizzes me after my first ride in public. Jim was a hard taskmaster but I owe him a great deal.

Proud father Paedar McCoy and myself after my first race at Phoenix Park. He travelled down from County Antrim specially for the race.

A big step . . . a happy occasion after I ride my first ever winner on the flat on Legal Steps at Thurles, in April, 1991.

Rizard (right) ploughs through the last obstacle, but is my first ever hurdle winner, at Gowran Park in April, 1994.

All dressed up for a photograph: the McCoy clan at sister Roisin's wedding to Diarmuid Shivers. Left to right: Paedar, Jane, mother Claire, Anne-Marie, Roisin, Diarmuid, Kelly, myself and Colm.

Two of my greatest mentors: Cullybackey trainer Billy Rock, who started me in horseracing, and Weyhill wizard Toby Balding, giving me instructions when I first came to England.

A Class of my own . . . Class of Ninetytwo gives me the then fastest ever 100 winners when scoring at Warwick on 21 November 1996, beating Peter Scudamore's record by 30 days.

Viking Flagship wins the Mumm Melling Chase at Aintree in March, 1996. At that stage this was the biggest win of my career.

Crash! Bang! Wallop! I came a right pearler at the last fence at Lingfield in March, 1996 from Brigadier Supreme with a race at my mercy. Luckily, the *Sporting Life*'s photographer Phil Smith snapped my disaster and then proved the hero of the hour as he dragged the horse away. I was pinned right underneath as my lights started to go out.

I beat champion hurdler Istabraq (left) on Pridwell at Aintree in April, 1998. I regarded it as my best riding display of the season, but the stewards didn't and I ended up with a six-day ban.

The man behind the mask! It's me in a crash helmet of a different kind when I took part in a charity go-kart meet at Wantage in March, 1998.

My first hurdle win came soon afterwards on Riszard at Gowran Park. He started warm favourite and won easily on really heavy ground.

In all I rode six flat and seven hurdle winners in Ireland, but I was beginning to get itchy feet. By now I was purely a jump jockey, and Jim Bolger did not have many jumpers, so I felt that there were not many opportunities for me in my native country. All the major jump yards had their retained first jockey, and I could see no vacancy signs outside any of the big stables.

The champion back then was Charlie Swan, the nicest chap you could ever meet. He was riding twice as many winners as anybody else and it was rightly claimed that he could take a six-month holiday each year and still be champion. I have always admired Charlie and to this day I have never heard him utter a single bad word about anybody. He is a great ambassador for Irish racing.

A game little horse who further put me on the map in Ireland before I left for England, was Huncheon Chance, trained in the north by Ian Ferguson – an old family friend – at Ballymena, just two miles from Billy Rock's Cullybackey stables. He was owned by County Antrim-based Tony McAleese. In all I rode Huncheon Chance six times: I won on him four times and was second and fifth. Huncheon is an area in County Antrim close to my home town, and Tony McAleese always named his horses with that prefix.

*　　*　　*

Ian Ferguson, who remains a good friend says that his day starts by opening the newspaper at the racing page to see what Tony is riding that particular day.

'I used to share my gallops with Billy Rock so that our horses could get used to different surroundings,' he explains. 'The first time I saw Tony McCoy he was only twelve years old and a titch of a thing. He was very small but I could see that he knew how to handle himself, and the horses. Billy Rock was very proud of his new discovery and often spoke warmly of "Wee Aunthnay". I used to have quite a few runners in the south of Ireland, and my lorry driver Tommy Smith and Tony McCoy became very friendly. When we had runners south of the border Tony often used to get lifts in our horse waggon to and from Jim Bolger's via the races. The wee fella was a quiet lad. He never said a whole lot. We used to meet him at the races and he always clued us in to what was going on. Even when he was a young apprentice jockey with Jim Bolger he seemed to know the stable buzzers. Some of his friends used to like to have a few quid on and Tony very seldom steered us in the wrong direction.

'He first rode for me back in April 1995, and then the last time in England was at Aintree in March 1996. I remember him always being a wee thing, so when he walked into the paddock at Liverpool that afternoon I could hardly recognise him. He seemed to have shot up in height and I was amazed by how much he had grown. It was as though somebody had stretched him. I am so thrilled to have been part of his life in the very early days. Back at home watching on TV we gave him a right roar when he won the Champion Hurdle on Make A Stand – I never saw a better natural hurdler in my life – and when he completed the double on Mr Mulligan two days later in the Gold Cup. I've told all my friends in Ballymena that in racing, a lad like this only comes along once in a lifetime.'

*   *   *

The winning connection with Ian Ferguson's Huncheon Chance started at Down Royal on 30 April 1995 when as a four-year-old he won a maiden hurdle when I was a seven pound claimer. Soon afterwards on 5 June 1995, we won a one-mile, six-furlong race on the flat at Sligo when I was claiming eight pounds. He won very easily that day. Fifteen days later we were just beaten in a hurdle race at Kilbeggan. I won a good few race notices when we then won a one-mile, six-furlong race again on the flat at Bellewstown on 7 July 1995. I thought I had the race won easily, but Celibate, then trained in Ireland by Mick O'Toole but later to join Charlie Mann at Lambourn, went up on me. I managed to conjure another run out of Huncheon Chance, however, and he just got up to win. It was a popular win, as connections like to have a few quid on. After I came to England, I flew back to Ireland one Sunday and won on Huncheon Chance again, this time over hurdles at Fairyhouse.

I was later to ride Huncheon Chance in the Oddbins Handicap Hurdle at the 1996 Grand National meeting at Aintree. Ian Ferguson has been a good friend and he is one of the biggest point-to-point trainers in the north. I'd have loved to have won on his horse at Aintree, but the ground was a bit quick for him and he had missed a bit of work beforehand.

Ian Ferguson did me another favour at an evening meeting at Dundalk. Northern Ireland trainer Tommy Miller was looking for a jockey for his hurdler Master Miller. He stressed that he needed a good, strong rider. Ian Ferguson put a good word in for me and I got the ride and duly won on him. These were small wins but they all helped to make my name.

I had developed my own riding style, probably started back in Northern Ireland when I was riding Billy Rock's point-to-pointers. I can say that I did not try to model my style on anybody, but at that stage Richard Dunwoody was my hero, and not just because he hailed, like me, from the north. Woody has his own style and there was no way I could copy him, but he was the rider I always liked to watch when Jim Bolger's lads were gathered round the TV in the staff canteen. If ever I am asked the best ride I consider I have seen from a jump jockey, I always say Richard Dunwoody on Wonder Man in the 1993 Arkle Chase at the Cheltenham Festival – when he was second. Jamie Osborne won the Arkle on Travado, but the ride Woody gave the one-length runner-up is one which should be shown to all young jockeys.

I spent many an hour in Jim Bolger's staff canteen watching the big races from England, and also paid the odd visit to a betting shop in Carlow, although I was, of course, not allowed to bet. I remember begging a pal to back Cool Ground in the 1992 Cheltenham Gold Cup and raising the roof in the betting shop when he came home at 25–1 for Adrian Maguire.

I was by now certain that my future lay in England. I had been friendly with the Northern Ireland trainer Paddy Graffin, and he was the first person I spoke to about riding in England when my second contract with Jim Bolger ran out.

I also mentioned to Listowel-based racing photographer Pat Healy that I was looking for a chance to make it in England. Pat was very friendly with Norman Williamson, who at that time was first jockey to Lambourn trainer Kim Bailey. For two or three weeks I was actually on standby to join Kim Bailey as his conditional jockey, but in the end the job went to Finbar Leahy, who eventually moved to the north of England.

The next big turning point in my life came at a Wexford meeting in July when I was chatting to Irish trainer and ex-jockey Eddie Harty. Eddie Harty is one of Ireland's greatest characters. He won the 1969 Grand National on Highland Wedding, trained by Toby Balding, who was to play the next big role in my life. I explained to Eddie that I did not think I had any future in Ireland.

Toby Balding was at Wexford that day, over on a holiday and at the same time looking at young horses. He had heard about me and was keen to meet me. Eddie came into the weighing-room and tapped me on the shoulder, saying, 'There is somebody here who wants to meet you.' I put on my jacket and went out to be introduced to Toby. Looking back, it was a pretty important meeting as it resulted in me going to England.

*   *   *

Eddie recalls, 'I had quite a few discussions with Tony, who at that stage had never ridden over fences in Ireland – or anywhere. I told him straight that he was a very good jockey and had a great future. Tony always had the brains to listen to you. He might not have said much but you could tell that every single word was sinking in. I'm thrilled that the little introduction went on to enhance his career all the way to the top. He has more than repaid my faith in him and promoting him to Toby Balding. Today Tony would without doubt stand amongst the greats. I was lucky enough to ride against Fred Winter and Terry Biddlecombe and Josh Gifford. Racing always needs stars and Tony McCoy shines as brightly as anybody who has jumped fences before him.

'He has also been a fine ambassador for Ireland with total dedication and not a hint of scandal. I was chatting to Mercy Rimell when she came over for the three-day festival at Punchestown in April 1997. We were discussing jump jockeys and she has a wealth of experience from all the great Rimell days at Kinnersley. She said, "This boy McCoy is very good over fences. He lets the horses flow over the fences. He lets the fences come to the horses and they become less of an obstacle." Mercy was dead right.

'Tony also has the natural knack of letting horses land running after jumping fences. That takes a lot of nerve and coolness. These jump jockeys are men apart. It is a completely uncompromising sport and very demanding. Tony is like the rest of them – they never moan.'

*   *   *

I left Ireland without ever riding in a chase, but within two weeks I was approached by Paddy Graffin to ride No Sir Rom in a chase at the Galway Festival. I popped back just for the Festival. Robert McCoubrey has had a lot of good horses over the years, including Strong Platinum. Paddy Graffin persuaded Robert McCoubrey that I was the youngster for the job, especially with my riding claim. I was quite nervous as I had not jumped a single fence since my days with Billy Rock. At Jim Bolger's stables my work had been purely with flat and hurdle horses. I jumped about five or six fences in that novice chase at Galway and then down I went. It wasn't a very bad fall and I was able to walk away. So, for the record books, my first hurdle ride in Ireland saw me being brought down at the second last, and in my first chase I was a faller. Hardly a great start.

*   *   *

Belfast owner, Robert McCoubrey recalls, 'When Paddy Graffin told me that he wanted to use this conditional jockey called Tony

McCoy at the Galway Festival, I had never heard of him. As this young kid walked into the paddock I can remember thinking, where did Paddy dig him up from? Tony was a bit reserved in those days and was, of course, unknown. That didn't last long, but when I first cast my eyes on him, I didn't know him from Adam. No Sir Rom was a very moderate horse. He was bought cheap . . . and he was sold cheap! It was in no way Tony's fault when he fell at Galway. Everybody always wants to know how Tony McCoy's first-ever ride over fences got his name. It's quite simple. He was purchased at the sales by a fellow called Morrison and it is his name spelt backwards.'

*		*		*

I plucked up courage to tell Jim Bolger that I was trying to get a job in England, and told him, 'Thank you for all your help, but I feel that it is best if I try and get a job across the water.'

Jim Bolger was not pleased. He said sharply, 'It shows how grateful you are to me, after all the help I have given you, that you should now throw it all in my face and walk away.' He tried to make me stay one more year and then think about going to England. Bolger realised that I was too heavy for the flat but wanted to see me get more experience in Ireland over hurdles, and later with jumpers. He felt that I was going along nicely and he had worked hard to create a jockey of me. Looking back, I suppose he did have a point, but I was young and very ambitious, and I couldn't see any future for me at Coolcullen.

To this day, despite all my quick success, Jim Bolger still reckons that I made a mistake by moving to England too soon. He's never admitted that I did the right thing, but my admiration for Jim Bolger is immense. He was not an easy man to please. He remains a one-off, and the experience at Coolcullen enabled me later to deal with Martin Pipe. They are very similar in so many ways. Like Martin Pipe, Jim Bolger has the great gift of being able to train bad horses. Any fool can train good horses – the real aces in racing are the ones who can train bad horses to win races. Jim Bolger is such a genius that he could train a goat to win a race.

*   *   *

After Tony clinched his second jockeys' title at the end of May 1997, Jim Bolger said, 'I remember Tony McCoy coming down to me on two weeks' trial. I always try and give any youngster a trial if I can. Tony was always well behaved and a decent, quiet-spoken lad. I liked his attitude from the first day he walked into my yard. He had plenty of go for one so young and inexperienced. Billy Rock had given him a big build-up but there was nothing else for me to have heard about him as he was still only fifteen years old. I recall that he wasn't that short. He was very narrow and still under seven stone. I have to say that in those early days he was a long way off the real thing. He had to work at it. But he soon showed that he had a good work ethic and attitude. Of course, at that time there was no way that we could have guessed that he was later going to get so big and heavy.

'I had no reason to have words with Tony McCoy. He was a very nice young man. After he had a winner or two he might have thought for a couple of weeks that he was suddenly a jockey of the future but we soon got him down to earth. He soon cottoned on to what the game is all about. If he fancied himself a bit, my head lad Pat O'Donavan would soon put him straight. You have to remember that this is probably the most important stage of anybody's life.

'When he went out to ride in his first-ever race on Nordic Torch at Phoenix Park on 1 September 1990, I gave him two important orders: look good and enjoy yourself. The horse wasn't much good and there was no way that I could fancy him. I would never put up a young rider for his first race on a horse that had a serious chance of winning. It was all part of Tony's introduction and it was just as important that he went into the weighing-room and mixed with top jockeys such as Christy Roche and Michael Kinane. It is quite an occasion for a jockey having his first ride. But basically they are just going through the motions.

'There is no genius in me in producing jockeys like Tony McCoy, Kevin Manning, Willie Supple, Paul Carberry and Dean Gallagher. I simply made sure everything was done right at this most important time of their lives. It is vital that youngsters like Tony have a proper attitude to life and to their fellow human beings. A headmaster may see his pupils from fifteen years old to seventeen but usually it is only from nine o'clock to three o'clock. I saw much, much more of my youngsters and was, I suppose, something of a foster father. I have a very strict no-smoking and no-drinking code of conduct. I succeeded on both counts, I'm delighted to say, with Tony.

'I was just hoping that he would not get too heavy as I didn't see his future at that stage as a jump jockey. But even allowing for his fall and the broken leg, he was getting heavier. Tony owes a lot to all my owners, men like Henryk de Kwiatkowski, who were quite happy to let my apprentices ride the very best horses, many with Classic potential, on the home gallops. The youngsters would get much more experience this way than simply trailing round the gaff tracks on outsiders.

'When Tony broke his leg it was a bad fall. Looking back, I suppose it could have been the finish of his career. To this day I still firmly believe that he should not have gone to England when he did. The fact that he got away with it does not mean that my view is incorrect. I was frightened that he could get a more serious fall and that really would have endangered his career. He was still very tall and brittle and I felt that he needed another year with us. He was like a matchstick and I stressed to him that he had no real protection if he had another serious fall.

'My honest opinion is that I felt I had done a lot for him, as had all the staff around him. He could have put something back into the place. I was thinking about Tony's physical condition and I really felt that he needed another year in Ireland. I also did not like the way he was approached by so-called farseeing people who thought that they could see he was going to be a future champion jump jockey.

'Wise scouts from across the Channel were said to have spotted his talents at Wexford and Gowran Park, but it was perfectly obvious to anybody that he sat well on a horse, rode especially well and had a bright future. He saw out his apprenticeship, finished his time and we shook hands.

'I feel that it was a decision Tony was lucky to get away with. He had virtually no chasing experience. If he had stayed with me he would have got stronger and wiser and would have been better equipped for the future. No doubt the results in England would have been just the same, but he didn't have to go when he still had his claim.

'It is the work riding at home that makes youngsters become successful jockeys. I expect that Tony got tired of my theory that the boss is always right, but I greatly enjoyed Tony's spell with me. If I could find another young man in his mould, I'd have him signed up fairly quickly. It was a great thrill to see his career take off in England and I watched with obvious pride when he won at Cheltenham on Make A Stand and Mr Mulligan.

'Any trainer who can see a youngster at fifteen years old and think that he will be a future champion is just daydreaming. I think in the last twenty years we have seen three outstanding jump jockeys in John Francome, Peter Scudamore and now Tony McCoy. But the trainer can only do so much. It is in the end down to the man. I expect there were times at Newmarket when Luca Cumani did not think that Frankie Dettori was going to scale the heights he has achieved. With Tony McCoy, Britain's gain was Ireland's loss.

'I still harbour some regrets at losing him. Irish racing would be better if Charlie Swan and Tony McCoy were involved against each other. At the end of the day, Tony has become a freelance in England so perhaps he could have done the same in Ireland, but I am sure that no matter what career he had turned to, Tony would have made a success. He is very clever. He is even smarter than Lester Piggott and would not make the same mistakes.'

CHAPTER 4

'You'll never be able to fill Peter Scudamore's boots'

Watching Tony McCoy dominating the jumping scene in England in 1997, it is hard to believe that he only arrived from his native Ireland in the summer of 1994. So much has been achieved in such a short time that the word meteoric is the only way to describe his sudden transformation from unknown conditional jockey to the present-day champion.

It was genial Weyhill trainer Toby Balding who fashioned the next vital stage of McCoy's career after his learning spell with Jim Bolger. Looking back, Toby Balding says, 'Amazing. That's the only way to label Tony's success. It is the unsung sporting achievement of the century. In golf everybody raves about Tiger Woods' rise to fame, but in racing Tony has gone from the bottom rung of the ladder to the very top in even more sensational style.

'He was very nearly the complete performer when he came to me, although at that stage he had very little experience of jumping and had not ridden in a single chase race. He got lucky, as he hit me at a time when I was on a good run. I had also lost Adrian Maguire to David Nicholson and didn't have a stable jockey. It all took off from there.

'I know that Tony's pride means he will want to continue as champion jockey for as long as he possibly can. I don't doubt that there are many more records he will smash along the way. From day one with me, when he came over from Ireland, I knew that he *was very special. Some jockeys are hopeless at assessing different horses, but Tony McCoy is bright.'*

C.D.

I came down to earth with a bang when I first walked into the jockeys' weighing-room at Stratford-on-Avon on Saturday, 13 August 1994 for my first ride in England. I did not have a valet, but Toby Balding's jockey Brian Clifford soon introduced me to John Buckingham of Foinavon fame. I'd seen film clips of his finest hour a hundred times and it was soon arranged that he would be my valet. For some reason, that day at Stratford I did not have any riding boots with me. John Buckingam's first words to me were: 'Borrow these. They are Peter Scudamore's old boots . . . You will never be able to fill Peter Scudamore's boots.' The remark took me back a bit as a nervous kid having his first ride in public in a new country, but John Buckingham was only trying to be friendly and his warm smile soon gave the game away. From that day on, virtually every afternoon of my life, Buck has been a great friend and ally. Everytime I change my colours and have my saddle weights altered – and that's every half an hour during our busy afternoons – Buck is there to help. It transpired that the boots were in fact an old pair of Scu's which he did not want when he retired in April 1993 after a fabulous career during which he was champion jockey for eight seasons. Coincidentally, Peter had a spell in Ireland with Jim Bolger and was then associated with Martin Pipe for the greater part of his career. I may never fill his boots, but at least we have ridden a very similar path.

John Buckingham must be the most remarkable Grand National-winning jockey of all time. Whenever people gather round to talk of the National, the name of the 1967 winner Foinavon always crops up. He won at 100–1, and will always be remembered for winning the Grand National when all the other runners fell.

John remains a totally modest personality, and you never hear him boast of the day he won the National. John only came into racing when his mother went to work at owner Edward Courage's Oxfordshire estate as a dairymaid. At fifteen John was given the choice of three jobs – as a shepherd on the farm, as a trainee gamekeeper, or in the stables. He had never even seen a horse, let alone sat on one.

It's strange to think that when I had my greatest moments of glory at the Cheltenham Festival in 1997 on Make A Stand and Mr Mulligan, it was Buck who handed me my silks and saddle . . . exactly thirty years after he achieved his never-to-be-forgotten moment of success on the completely unfancied Foinavon.

The horse was such an unlikely big-race winner that Foinavon's trainer John Kempton wasn't even at Aintree, and went instead to Worcester to ride a winner, Three Donds. The owner stayed away as well, and watched Foinavon's unbelievable win on television.

John was the sixth jockey to ride Foinavon that famous season. The National was the Anne, Duchess of Westminster reject's sixteenth race of the season with no previous wins.

*   *   *

Now John Buckingham recalls, 'When the field approached the twenty-third fence – the one after Becher's and the smallest on the circuit – I was about a hundred yards behind the leaders. We got over the fence at a canter and then just kept galloping on to win the National. It was all so unexpected that I didn't even have any digs in Liverpool the night before, and ended up squeezing into my brother Tom's boarding house and sleeping on two armchairs pulled together. It wasn't the best night's sleep before riding in the Grand National.

'I should have guessed that the riding of Foinavon in the Grand National was going to be a bit special – John Kempton phoned me the Wednesday before the big race just as I was getting dressed to go to my uncle's funeral. Now, there's hardly a day when there is not a mention of Foinavon.

'I have been a valet since August 1971, and it was a great stroke of luck when Tony McCoy became one of my boys. It seems that in the valet game, when you get a jockey, you get him for the rest of his riding life. I hope that's the case with Tony. He is brilliant. So easy to deal with. If he asks for something special, it's as though he is putting us out.

'Often, he'll ask rather shyly if it is okay for him to use a different pair of boots. He's superb to work with. His courage after falls is quite remarkable. I remember one day my brother Tom, who works with me, rang me to say, "AP won't be riding tomorrow. He's had a bad fall and hurt his wrist." When I got to the races the next day Tony was there and asked me if I could loosen his shirt button as his wrist hurt. I willingly did so, only for Tony to go off to get passed fit to ride that day by the doctor. How he did it I will never know. He couldn't even pull a sleeve over his riding glove, but he went out and rode two winners that afternoon, including one in a driving finish, when he kept having to change his whip hand. I watched the race on the TV in the jockeys' changing-room and couldn't believe it. When he got dressed to go home I had to fasten all his buttons!

'He's very much like John Francome – very laid back. He's always the same and he's not a bighead. Fame hasn't altered him at all from the same lad I helped on his first day's riding at Stratford. No matter what success he gets, I'm sure he'll always be the same modest chap. What I admire most about him is that he is level-headed and doesn't alter according to his results. Steve Smith-Eccles was one of my jockeys; he would give me a right bollocking one day when things didn't go right, and then be Prince Charming the next day when he'd ridden a couple of winners. He was never the same two days running.

'Of course, there are occasions when Tony can get a little agitated. The big boys are out there playing for big stakes and the pressure is bound to get to them on occasions, but I have never seen him come back in a rage and chuck the saddle on the table like some jockeys.

'Tony remains the most dedicated jockey in the weighing-room. I do, indeed, hope to be his valet for the rest of his riding career.'

*   *   *

I had been at Toby Balding's stables for only a couple of weeks when my first rides in England were lined up for me by Dave Roberts, who was to become my full-time agent. Dave has been a close friend of Toby Balding's for a long time and it was always on the cards that I should join his string of jockeys. Like John Buckingham, Dave Roberts has been with me from day one and I couldn't be happier with the arrangement.

It was through my contact with Northern Ireland trainer Paddy Graffin and Belfast owner Robert McCoubrey that I secured my first two rides in England that afternoon at Stratford. Paddy had mentioned to Mr McCoubrey that I had left Jim Bolger's stables in Ireland and was trying to make a go of it in England. The fact that I had already fallen on his No Sir Rom at Galway did not seem to alter Mr McCoubrey's agreement that I should yet again ride in his colours.

*   *   *

Robert McCoubrey recalls, 'When Tony McCoy came to England I was keen to put him up on my horses, which were trained by John Jenkins. I should have retained Tony McCoy myself from day one in England. I would have made a nice few bob out of him. You can say that he was the one who got away.'

*   *   *

My first ride in England was on Arctic Life in the Clifford Chambers Novices' Hurdle at Stratford. Adrian Maguire had already ridden him twice before during that season for John Jenkins, when the five-year-old had been third at Bangor-on-Dee and second at Worcester. He was a consistent sort but no world beater, and I finally finished second on him, beaten easily by twelve lengths by Darren O'Sullivan on the 6–4 on favourite Wilkins. I didn't think that I had done too much wrong, and later in the afternoon I rode another for Robert McCoubrey when finishing last of four on Crews Castle in the Fisher Quality Foods Handicap Hurdle, which was won by Peter Hobbs on his brother Philip Hobbs' Badastan.

My first day saw no winners, but I felt that I had made a good start. At least I had earned enough from my two riding fees to buy my own riding boots and I could return the kind loan of Peter Scudamore's old boots to John Buckingham.

Dave Roberts wasted little time in getting me my third ride, and I was lined up to ride Omidjoy for John Jenkins in the St Peter-St James Hospice Handicap Hurdle at Plumpton on 29 August 1994. Again I was in the Robert McCoubrey colours on the Irish-bred Omidjoy . . . and again I finished second. This time I was beaten six lengths by Adrian Maguire on Heretical Miss, who was the 2–1 on favourite. This was a modest seller and there were only four runners. John Jenkins seemed happy with my riding. I was amazed by the Plumpton track the first time I saw it and I was interested to learn from the senior jockeys that the great Fred Winter detested the little Sussex track so much he vowed to his outstanding guv'nor Ryan Price that he would never ride there again. It was a good day for Dave Roberts, though, as Adrian Maguire, very much his star man at the time, rode five winners out of six that afternoon at Plumpton. Adrian won the first five races, only to have to pull up Drama Critic in the last race.

*   *   *

John Jenkins says, 'I was delighted to give Tony McCoy his first three rides in England. Robert McCoubrey told me all about him and I knew that if he wanted him in the saddle, he would be the business. Even then Tony had his heart in the game and was very determined. He was always trying his very hardest and it's a hallmark which we can all see today. Where I was lucky was that in those days I was using him with a seven-pound advantage as he was still a seven-pound claimer. Just imagine using him now and claiming. He'd be unbeatable!'

*   *   *

Moving from Jim Bolger to Toby Balding was like switching from one world to another. In County Carlow, Jim Bolger ruled his yard with a rod of iron. He was feared by his staff and several lads did not stay for very long, but at Fyfield, near Weyhill in Hampshire, the atmosphere in the stables was completely different. Toby Balding was far more laid back about the business of training horses. I enjoyed the set-up at Toby's far more because it was a jump yard and I found it far more exciting. I was on trial at Fyfield for the first two weeks, but when I signed up I enjoyed good digs in nearby Ludgershall.

The stable stars at that time were two ex-Champion Hurdlers – Morley Street and Beech Road. It was a great thrill to ride two horses who had won the big hurdling prize at Cheltenham. Beech Road was a bit of a character – later on, one day at Liverpool, he went completely on strike with me at the start. He just got into one of his moods and refused to budge. He would not go anywhere until I got off his back. As we say back in Ireland . . . he got notions.

Morley Street was another character, although when I joined the stables in midsummer 1994, he had probably seen better days. It was still marvellous to ride a horse of that ability, and just riding him on the gallops was a pleasure. He was so big and strong that I can say I haven't sat on many nicer horses, before or since. If I was asked to name the best riding display I have seen at Aintree it would without doubt be Graham Bradley's cheeky win on Morley Street in the 1993 Martell Hurdle, which he won for the fourth year in succession. The way Graham Bradley played cat and mouse with the others up the run-in was quite brilliant, although I suppose he would have been in deep trouble with everybody – including the stewards – if it had gone wrong.

Those early days in England were a great thrill . . . apart from finding the racecourses. I never actually turned up late for meetings, although there were some close shaves. Toby would give me maps and instructions but I often got lost. They were all new roads to me. Bangor-on-Dee and Uttoxeter took a few attempts before I actually found the tracks. I can also remember circling around Sedgefield for quite some time.

I had my first ride for Toby Balding on Southampton in the Garrick Jubilee Challenge Cup Handicap Hurdle at Stratford-on-Avon on 3 September 1994. Southampton, a leggy gelding, had been a good servant to Toby Balding and had won his previous race at Cartmel on 27 August, when he landed a bit of a touch down to 2–1 favourite. This time he started 7–2, and the warm favourite at 3–1 was Saivez, ridden by Norman Williamson. On the run-in I thought that Southampton would win but we were just touched off by a short head. As there had been a hint of interference I was persuaded to object to the winner. This was my first visit to the stewards' room; but not I'm afraid for the last time, I came off second best with the stewards and Norman Williamson was allowed to keep the race, although he was stood down for two days for excessive use of the whip.

I loved my new life in England. Visiting new tracks was exciting, but from my first four rides, I had finished second three times. I was beginning to feel that I was suffering from seconditis. There is no worse feeling than to be a close second. It did cross my mind whether I was ever going to get my name down next to a winner in England, but I should have known that I could rely on Dave Roberts getting me going.

I was soon to strike lucky with a horse trained by a village blacksmith. My first-ever winner in England was a remarkable six-year-old mare called Chickabiddy, trained by Gordon Edwards, an enthusiastic permit holder from Wheddon Cross, near Minehead in Somerset. Just twenty-four days after my English debut on runner-up Arctic Life at Stratford-on-Avon, Chickabiddy was entered for the William Hill Diamond Jubilee Handicap Hurdle at Exeter, worth the sum of £718 to the winner. Dave Roberts had struck up quite a good working relationship with Gordon Edwards over the years, and persuaded him that he had a good seven-pound claimer who might fill the bill. Chickabiddy was out of the handicap and an unfancied 7–1 shot in the six-runner race, but she jumped the real hurdles well and I was able to drive her out to beat Simon McNeill on Just Rosie by a length. Gordon Edwards was thrilled by the victory and I, of course, was delighted to win my first race in England. Chickabiddy was only a little mare but I have fond memories of her getting me on the scoreboard.

* * *

Gordon Edwards' wife Angela says, 'My husband has always combined his job of blacksmith with training a few horses of our own under permit. It's purely a hobby and we have to get all the training done before eight o'clock each morning when Gordon goes to work. We had never heard of Tony McCoy when Dave Roberts rang to recommend him, but over the years Dave Roberts has been very useful to us and we value his opinion. Tony was a very shy lad when he walked into the paddock. He was so shy that he didn't really like to look you in the face, but he gave Chickabiddy a marvellous ride and did everything that Gordon told him. He listened and then he went out and did the business. Needless to say, we love using Tony McCoy whenever we can and it's obviously no fluke that he went on to become conditional champion that season and then full senior champion for the next two seasons. We are proud that our little mare was his first winner in England.'

* * *

It was on Gordon Edwards' Little Hooligan at Taunton that I had my first big brush with officialdom after being first past the post in the Orchard Portman Handicap Selling Hurdle on 9 November 1995. Five jockeys went the wrong side of a hurdle, which had been dolled off for stricken rider Michael Clarke. We all received a seven-day ban for our alleged misjudgement, which was quite ridiculous. I had thought we'd all get a fine. I was very angry at the time as I believed it could have cost me the championship. Jamie Osborne was the one who came away laughing, and he kept chirping, 'It plainly says on a notice in the weighing-room that when a hurdle is dolled off, you always go to the left.' That was all very well but at the time when I approached the fence the flagmen were just waving their flags, and didn't seem to know which way they were directing us. It was a shambles. We lost the appeal against the seven-day bans, although the appeal money of £240 was refunded.

I was extremely annoyed to pick up two separate whip bans at the Galway Festival. I finished second on both horses. I was furious. I told the press lads that I would never ride in my home country again, which was obviously a bit of an exaggeration. However, at the Punchestown Festival in 1996 I won on Mayasta (5–1), Shaunies Lady (10–1) and Have To Think (8–1). I won £2,000 first prize for being top jockey at the meeting. That was a real bonus as I missed the first day of the meeting altogether and had only really been persuaded to come over to Ireland to ride Lord Dorcet, who finished third in the big novice chase.

Tuesday, 4 October 1994 was an eventful day in my life: my first-ever riding double, and a bit of a bollocking from a trainer. Racing is full of things that happened, or might have happened, but this was a day when luck was on my side. For the Old Saw Mill Conditional Jockeys' Handicap Chase at Newton Abbot, Johnny Supple was due to ride Bonus Boy for Bridport, Dorset trainer Bob Buckler. Unfortunately for Johnny Supple, his car broke down on the way to Newton Abbot and he was not able to ride. Bob Buckler was away at Malvern horse sales and his wife Nell was left with the task of finding a replacement conditional jockey. The lad they had in mind was not able to do the weight, and Brendan Powell, who rode regularly for the stable, put a word in for me.

Bonus Boy was an ex-point-to-pointer who did not stay three miles. He had no decent form at all and started the eight-horse race as a 20–1 outsider. Other horses fell in the race and I was left clear two fences from home. He made a big mistake at the last fence and I was lucky not to be unshipped, but he showed a good turn of foot from the last and I was able to win by five lengths to record my first-ever chase victory in England. It was hardly an inspiring event and there was no bid for Bonus Boy, who had won for the only time in his life. He did not win again, as sadly he fell later in the season, also at Newton Abbot, and broke his back. I was very chuffed to win on Bonus Boy but the race was not without a spot of bother afterwards.

* * *

Bob Buckler says, 'I had never heard of Tony McCoy when my wife rang me on my mobile phone at the horse sales and said that she had engaged this youngster. I listened to the race via my phone and was delighted when we won. However, I was less than pleased when I heard afterwards that Tony McCoy had jumped off the horse in the winners' enclosure, not said a single word to my wife or the owners, and dashed into the weighing-room. The next time I spoke to Dave Roberts I told him that I thought it was a poor show, and pointed out that this was not the way to behave. If I had known that Tony McCoy was going to go on to become champion jockey I might have thought differently.'

Bob Buckler trains from his five-hundred-acre farm set in deepest Dorset. He was a regular on the West Country point-to-point circuit and ran a small livery yard with his farm. With the encouragement of Peter Jones, now head of the Tote, he decided to take out a trainer's licence. He trained his first winner when Aviation Support won at Newton Abbot on 3 August 1991. Bob has always done well, with around thirty National Hunt horses, although he admits that being so far from any track is a problem – 'Wincanton is our nearest and we have to travel long distances to other courses.' He rode thirty-four point-to-point winners himself and does exceptionally well with his gallops in between his happily grazing sheep and cattle.

There may have been a little rumpus over Tony's first chase winner, but Bob now says, 'It all ended happily. I was having a drink in the bar at the races when Toby Balding came in with this youngster. Obviously the news of my conversation with Dave Roberts had gone back to Toby, as he came over and introduced me to the lad, saying, "This is Tony McCoy, who you wanted to see to give a bollocking to." Tony grinned and said sorry, we had a drink, and the incident was soon forgotten. I am delighted to say that I'm chuffed to have given Tony his first chase winner, and he has ridden for me several times since, notably when Well Briefed won a conditional jockey handicap chase at Cheltenham on 9 December 1994. My one regret with Bonus Boy's one win at 20–1 was that I didn't back him. I suppose with the then unknown future champion jockey on board I should have made my fortune.'

*   *   *

I'm sorry that I upset Mr Buckler and I realise that trainers and owner's connections always want to know how I think their horses have run, but it was an unexpected spare ride. You live and learn. In the very next race I was due to partner Ask The Governor for Toby Balding, who I could see waiting anxiously for me to change into the different colours. Luckily, this had a happy ending as well, as I won the South Wales Shower Supplies Rada Faucets Handicap Hurdle by a neck from previous winner Beam Me Up Scotty. What made that win even more exciting for me was that I beat Richard Dunwoody and Adrian Maguire, who were back in third and fourth.

In my first season as a conditional jockey it was Ask The Governor and Southampton who really put me on the map for Toby Balding. I thought I had a win in the bag at Wincanton on 6 October on the John White-trained Sharp Swing, until Richard Dunwoody came flying by me on McGillycuddy Reeks, trained by Martin Pipe. Not for the first or last time I marvelled at the skill of Woody . . . and a certain trainer called Martin Pipe.

Everybody in jumping knows that Cheltenham is the Mecca of the sport. Even as a kid I used to hear of the annual trip to the Festival from Irish racing fans. I was lucky enough to have a winner with my first ride at the outstanding Gloucestershire track. That win came on 29 September 1994, when I won the Frenchie Nicholson Conditional Jockeys' Handicap Hurdle on Wings of Freedom, a little horse trained by John Jenkins at Royston. My 10–1 shot was always going well and I led on the run-in up the hill to hold off Glenn Tormey on Borrowed And Blue to win by a neck. My second ride at Cheltenham was also a winner, when I scored on the Gary Moore-trained Bo Knows Best at 13–2 in the Eagle Pests Control Handicap Hurdle on 7 October. It was an easy victory and Bo Knows Best came home unchallenged by eleven lengths.

By Christmas 1994, I had gone clear in the race for the conditional jockeys' title. When I started riding in England, Rodney Farrant had already ridden thirteen winners, and Philip Hide was not far behind him. Toby Balding by now had visions of me being the champion conditional jockey. He had already secured the title for his previous top young rider, Adrian Maguire.

My association with Martin Pipe has accounted for so many winners, but none of my success in England would have been possible without the help and guidance of Toby Balding. Everybody knows that it was Toby who offered me a job in England and arranged everything when I came over. I shall forever be in his debt.

When I arrived at Weyhill I had not done a lot of riding over fences, in fact I had never won a race over the bigger obstacles, but joining a top National Hunt yard meant that I was able to ride top-class jumpers every morning on the gallops.

I like Toby a lot. He's straight and a great trainer with the right tackle. His past successes include winning the Grand National in 1969 and 1989 with Highland Wedding and Little Polveir. In recent years, however, he has not had the sort of owners who can go out and spend large sums of money on horses. There seems to be a theory that he is a bit of a ducker and a diver, planning big gambling coups. If that's so, I've been left out of the plot! When my housemate Barry Fenton was had up for a non-trier, Toby was quick to point out that he had enjoyed such a bad spell of luck that it was winners he was desperately after, not non-triers.

It's so difficult to keep all my trainers and owners happy, but I owe Toby a big vote of thanks. His loyalty is something that I will not forget. Of course, there has been a bit of friction from both sides when I have chosen a horse of Martin Pipe's over one of Toby's and vice versa.

*   *   *

Genial and generous, Toby Balding has been training at Weyhill since he took over at the age of twenty-one after his father's death in 1957. A larger than life character, Toby has been a great teacher in his time: David Elsworth, Jim Old, Michael Kauntze, Charlie Brooks, Ian Balding and Peter Makin are amongst his ex-pupils.

At the end of the 1996–7 campaign, and shortly before he had his first Royal Ascot winner on the flat with 20–1 Sea Freedom, Balding said, 'I am thrilled to be the man who got Tony McCoy to come to England. I was on a horse-buying trip to Ireland, but a very good contact said, "Don't worry about horses, watch this kid McCoy." The horse he rode at Wexford got beaten, but I had seen enough. He came on two weeks' trial and has been with me ever since. Tony's ability speaks for itself. He has an uncanny knack of always being in the right place in a race at the right time. He is a brilliant race-reader, can work out his tactics in a split second, and still be so very stylish. But at the same time he can hand out a few whacks if he has to. It is very hard to liken him to other jockeys. He has the natural flair and cheek of John Francome, the obviously commanding horsemanship of Richard Dunwoody, but can be like an inspired Lester Piggott, riding with great force from the last obstacles.

'Actually, if I had to liken him to any one rider it would have to be David Mould. He is sheer class, but beneath it all there is a character of steel. I am so pleased that despite all his success he is still the same quiet lad I met at Wexford a few years ago. Success hasn't changed him one bit. He may be teetotal, but there have been many occasions when we've had a few drinks to celebrate his winners.'

*   *   *

Toby was very good to me and took a lot of time to tell me what I was doing right – and wrong. He paid a lot of attention to detail, and watched all my races on SIS, whether I was riding for him or getting outside rides. He was the first to tell me if I was doing something wrong. I realised how lucky I was to have been involved with first a top Irish flat trainer and now a leading English jump trainer.

Toby's lads were all great fun and there was a fine spirit in the yard. I would muck out horses, ride two lots and then dash off to faraway places I had never seen before to ride in races, and Toby gave me every encouragement.

By now my little Peugeot 205 van was getting to know virtually all the jump tracks in Britain.

Adrian Maguire still rode for us when he was not required for David Nicholson, and most of the other big rides at that time went to Jamie Railton and Jimmy Frost. By now, though, the newspapers were aware of A. P. McCoy and the fact that I was going for the junior title. Everybody began to compare me with Adrian Maguire, although it was hard to liken us, as Adrian is 5ft 5in and I am much taller at nearly 5ft 11in.

By the turn of the year all eyes are firmly fixed on the Cheltenham Festival in March and I was beginning to pencil in a few horses whom I might be lucky enough to partner in my first full season in England. When I won on Supreme Master at Ascot on 8 February, Chepstow trainer Miss Clair Johnsey told me that she wanted me to partner the five-year-old at the Festival, and so he duly became my first ride at the season's biggest meeting. We started at 100–1 for the Citroën Supreme Novices' Hurdle. I was going well to about halfway, but then we started to weaken and eventually finished sixteenth of nineteen behind the Irish-trained Tourist Attraction, ridden by Mark Dwyer. I also teamed up with another woman trainer, Jackie Retter, for my second ride on the same day of the Festival. I had won on Mrs Retter's Leavenworth at Sandown in February, and he took his chance in the Astec Vodaphone Gold Card Handicap Hurdle Final. He was a 33–1 outsider and was never sighted back in eighth behind the short-head winner Miracle Man.

I shall never forget the atmosphere of Cheltenham for my first Festival.

As I was by no means a top-flight jockey at this stage of my career, I did not attract any rides on the second day of the Cheltenham Festival and journeyed to Nottingham for the Wednesday fixture. The day started badly when I was tailed off on Breckenbrough Lad in the first race, then I was tenth on Toby Balding's Conti d'Estruval and third on Jeff King's Fortunes Course in a handicap hurdle. I did manage to win the Get In Free Today Handicap Chase on The Boiler White for Tim Thomson Jones, before being unplaced on the same trainer's Charming Girl. After the excitement of the first day of the Cheltenham Festival, the joys of Nottingham did seem a little dull.

I was ready on the Thursday for my first ride in the Cheltenham Gold Cup on 100–1 outsider Beech Road. I had won on the ex-Champion Hurdler at Cheltenham the previous January when we thrashed Jumbeau by fifteen lengths as 14–1 outsiders in a good field, which included Martin Pipe's subsequent Grand National runner-up Encore Un Peu. Beech Road's owners, Mr and Mrs Tony Geake, were keen to let him have his chance in the Gold Cup and I was thrilled to have a ride in the big race. Over the years, far worse horses than Beech Road had lined up in the Gold Cup. I was delighted when Toby Balding greeted me in the paddock before the race with the words: 'Go out and enjoy yourself.' I guess I was the only jockey that day to be given the freedom of those pre-race instructions. Beech Road finished seventh, although I did finish in front of the 1993 Gold Cup hero Jodami.

Earlier that afternoon I had what I considered my first real chance of a Cheltenham Festival winner when Toby Balding's Brave Tornado ran as 10–1 fourth favourite in the Daily Express Triumph Hurdle. This small, sturdy gelding had previously won at Newbury, Exeter and Cheltenham and was a big whisper in our yard to go very close. Twenty-six runners went to post for this annual cavalry charge, but Brave Tornado's chance was completely wrecked at the very first flight of hurdles. Lady's Vision, trained in Ireland by Pat Flynn and ridden by Kevin O'Brien, fell at the first obstacle and Brave Tornado and I were badly hampered. I was nearly knocked on to the deck and we stopped to a near walk and were stone last as they went by the stands on the first circuit. Brave Tornado was actually flying in the closing stages and we made rapid progress from two flights out, but there was no way we could reach the leaders.

In the end we reached a very respectable seventh, behind Martin Pipe's 16–1 winner Kissair. I still believe that Brave Tornado would have gone close to winning but for that first-flight mishap. He had a really big chance, especially after the way he had previously won the Finesse Hurdle at Cheltenham for me, when he easily beat Clifton Beat by four lengths.

I often bumped into Martin Pipe at the races and he always gave me a friendly nod, although at that stage I don't think he knew me from Adam. You can imagine my delight when he contacted me and offered me the ride on Chatam in the Martell Grand National on 8 April 1995. I had never ridden for him before in a big race and I had no experience whatsoever over the big Liverpool fences. As a claiming jockey, it was quite some-thing for the champion trainer to place his faith in me in this way. Chatam had won the 1991 Hennessy Gold Cup at New-bury, when ridden by Peter Scudamore. At the age of eleven, Chatam had become a quirky old so-and-so, but he was still a class act on his day and a good first ride for me to have in the Grand National.

The build-up for the National is tremendous, and I had to pinch myself to believe that I was actually riding in a race seen world-wide by a television audience of over 800 million. Sadly, there was no fairytale National debut for me, and Chatam fell at the twelfth fence, which is the second fence and ditch after Valentine's. At least I had the thrill of flying over Becher's Brook successfully for the first time in my life, even though we were to fall six fences further on. The twelfth fence, which doubles up as the twenty-eighth on the second circuit, is the only jump on the Liverpool course with the ditch on the far side of the obstacle. Its other claim to fame is that it is the last fence before the runners on the second circuit reach the Melling Road, and is always referred to as the 'third from home'.

My first National was won by fellow Irishman Jason Titley on Royal Athlete. Jason is probably the only jockey to have to undergo a breath test before riding in the National. Jenny Pitman, who trained Royal Athlete, told him that she would smell his breath on the morning of the race, and if she detected any whiff of alcohol, he'd be sacked. Happily, Jason survived the breath test . . . and the thirty obstacles.

Riding at my first Aintree meeting was not a great success as my first ride, Eskimo Nell trained by John Spearing, fell three out in the Glenlivet Anniversary Hurdle. The ground was much too firm for Brave Tornado when we finished sixth in the Martell Mersey Novices' Hurdle on the eve of the Grand National, the same day that cussed old Beech Road downed tools at the start of the Perrier Jouet Handicap Chase and refused to race. I was always behind and finished eleventh in the final race of the meeting on Gowlaun in the boys' event. Nevertheless, I was now well on the way to building up an unassailable lead in the race for the conditional jockeys' title.

Dave Roberts did a brilliant job in my first season in England, and with Toby Balding's great help I eventually clinched the conditional jockeys' title. My last winner of the season was on Martin Pipe's Crosula at Hereford on 1 June 1995, when there was much talk that all was not going well between Martin Pipe and Richard Dunwoody. Richard Dunwoody was injured that day after a bad fall from James Pigg, trained by Martin Pipe, in the Edwardian Selling Handicap Chase, and it was clear that he would not be able to ride Crosula in the next race but one, the Stoke Edith Novices' Hurdle.

In the weighing-room fellow Irishman Brendan Powell, a real jokester, was having a field day and taking imaginary bets on who would get the call-up for Crosula and then be invited to be the champion trainer's new stable jockey. It was real end-of-season messing about, and Brendan made me the favourite. When one of the valets shouted that Mr Pipe wanted to speak to Tony McCoy, the weighing-room erupted with laughter. I had to keep a straight face and happily accepted the ride on Crosula.

In typical Martin Pipe style, Crosula made every yard. We were always well clear and we won unchallenged, as 6–4 second favourite behind the 4–5 favourite Henry Cone, who came third for Warren Marston and trainer David Nicholson. It was my last winner of my first championship season – and also probably my easiest.

*   *   *

Beating Adrian Maguire's 1991–2 record of seventy-one wins as a conditional jockey, when winning on Pennine Pass in the Dugie Mack Selling Handicap Chase at Fontwell on 29 May, made Tony McCoy the most successful conditional rider ever. Pennine Pass, who was backed from 6–4 to evens, was always in the leading group, and after setting out on the second circuit of the figure-of-eight course, stayed on gamely to win by ten lengths from Achiltibuie. Dave Roberts was having a rare day away from his desk and form-books and said, 'McCoy is not bad for a boy who has only been here for a year and had not ridden over fences before he got to England.'

Tony went on that day to score a 6–1 double for trainer Dai Williams on Symbol Of Success in the Chris and Nicky Breakfast Show Juvenile Novices' Hurdle. After the race, Williams said, 'Tony McCoy is so switched on as to what is happening in a race.'

He had also received a pat on the back in the *Sporting Life* after winning on Mistress Rosie in the Arrow Maiden Claiming Hurdle at Hereford on 13 February. Winning trainer Jackie Retter said, 'That's only the second ride Tony McCoy has had for me, but on that showing he is the finished article. He's so polished through-out a race and is surely a champion jockey in the making.' It was a welcome change of luck for the West Country trainer as she had gone over a month since her last winner, Karicleigh Lad, at Exeter on 2 January.

*   *   *

My first season in England ended at Stratford-on-Avon on 3 June 1995, the very same track where it had all started for me the previous year on 13 August. Thanks to Dave Roberts I had 475 rides to get my championship-winning score of seventy-four. My nearest rival was Philip Hobbs with thirty-four winners.

It had been a long, hard season, and I now enjoyed a good rest . . . all four days of it. One season ended at Stratford-on-Avon on Saturday, 3 June and I was back in action for the start of summer jumping at Perth on Thursday, 8 June. Quite a holiday!

CHAPTER 5

Dave Roberts – special agent

An elegant town house, tucked away in the leafy Surrey hills between Redhill and Reigate, is the secret mission control of Tony McCoy's meteoric climb to the top of the jump jockeys' profession. This is the home of Dave Roberts, Tony McCoy's special agent and the man solely responsible for booking all his rides since he came to England. In three seasons Roberts has provided the Irishman with all the ammunition to clinch one conditional jump jockeys' title and two full senior titles.

Once, Roberts' stables had fourteen jockeys and he was dubbed special agent 0014 – twice as powerful as fiction's James Bond. However his mini army now consists of Tony McCoy, Adrian Maguire, Norman Williamson, Mick Fitzgerald, Richard Johnson, Richard Guest, John Kavanagh, Dean Gallagher, Robert and Andrew Thornton, Graham Bradley and Barry Fenton. Roberts jokes, 'I have got a better squad than Glenn Hoddle. Throughout a season I shall be booking over four thousand rides.' Modest Roberts is the Goldfinger of agents. He cops ten per cent of all his jockeys' riding fees, plus ten per cent of all their winnings. What does he earn? 'That's something only my accountant and I know,' smiles Roberts.

'But my relationship with Tony McCoy is more than a business one. We have become close friends, although I have never been to his house and he has never been to mine. Too busy. I am still

*waiting for the party to celebrate his first conditional jockeys'
title. Our success has been built on mutual respect. I admit that I
haven't missed a trick with this fella. The first day I met him at
Plumpton, Adrian Maguire rode the first five winners on the card.
Tony said to me, "Jeez, I'd love to do that." Well, the five winners
came in 1997 at Uttoxeter and Newton Abbot. What Tony has
achieved in three seasons is incredible, and the nicest part of the
job is that there is not an ounce of conceit in Tony.*

'*Getting Tony to praise himself is impossible. You have to
bludgeon any self-praise out of him. I watched on SIS when he
won on Martin Pipe's Doualago at Aintree on a Friday night
fixture on 16 May 1997. Doualago was off the bridle throughout
the entire second circuit and Tony produced a great performance
to overcome mistakes and beat Russ Garritty on Micky Ham-
mond's Bas de Laine. It was a sensational riding display, but when
Tony and I chatted on the phone, I asked him if he thought it was
an exceptional win. Tony simply replied, "I just got lucky."*

'*Garritty, a blunt-talking Yorkshireman, said, "There's no
other jockey in the world who would have won on that bugger
tonight apart from Tony McCoy."*'

*Roberts is a serious character, and is rarely seen mingling with
racecourse crowds. From the crack of dawn he is ringing round
from his control module to arrange McCoy's rides. His brain is a
form-book and he knows all the dangerous jumpers on the circuit.
His union with Tony McCoy has become the most successful
jockey–agent combination the jumping game has ever known.*

C.D.

T here is no way that I could be champion jockey without the
assistance of Dave Roberts as my agent. Ever since I came to
England he has done a quite remarkable job sorting out all my
rides. One day I will take time off to work out the share of my
earnings and prize money he has earned since he took over my

rides, although I know that he is worth every penny. His dedication to his job is something else, and I know that I can always rely on him to put my best interests first.

It was also a stroke of luck for me when I teamed up with Ronnie Beggan, the former successful National Hunt jockey, and his business partner Cameron McMillan. Since the start of the 1996–7 season, RBI Promotions Ltd have handled all of my promotional work. Once the season gets underway I am so busy that I often have to ring Dave Roberts to find out where I am riding the next day – and which horses! I could not be more happy with Dave Roberts. He arranges all the rides, while Ronnie and Cameron see to the sponsorship side of affairs. They lined up the deals with Blue Thunder sports clothing, the *Sun*, and then the tie-up with Guinness, which in the end saw me galloping up the hill to win the Cheltenham Gold Cup with the famous Irish stout logo on my blue silks.

In three seasons he has booked all my rides, and I can't recall an angry word between us. In all that time I think the only controversy arose when Dave booked me a ride at Bangor. On the morning of the race Toby Balding looked up the horse's form and told me, 'You're not going there just to ride that one!'

Dave's biggest asset is his brain, which doubles up as a walking form-book. You only have to mention some obscure chaser and he will straightaway be able to tell you its form going back for two or three seasons. This way he is able to avoid booking me on dodgy jumpers.

In my early days it was often Dave Roberts who introduced me to trainers who hadn't a clue who I was, and he gradually built up a list of trainers who kept me busy.

Over the years Dave has been able to keep all my main trainers happy – at least nearly all of the time. When you ride as a freelance there are bound to be races where more than one trainer wants your services. That's when Dave is good at working out exactly which horse has the best chance of winning. Keeping all the various owners happy is also an art. It must be annoying for owners if I ride a winner for them in one race, only to get up to beat them in a later race.

I don't think I had been in England for more than two days before I was contacted by Dave Roberts, and he has been my right-hand man ever since. We speak every day, but very seldom meet. He sometimes pops down to Plumpton, or comes to Ascot or Kempton, but usually he is far too busy to leave his office. I don't honestly know what I would do without him.

*   *   *

Ever-modest Dave Roberts says, 'Frightening. That's the only word to describe what Tony McCoy has achieved since he came to England. I thought that what Adrian Maguire achieved when he came over from Ireland was pretty exceptional, but Tony's record of being conditional champion and then twice full champion in his first three years will probably never be emulated. I can't see his record being matched in my lifetime. In just three years he is nearly halfway to riding 1,000 winners. Barring serious injury, Tony will surely beat Peter Scudamore's record of 1,678 career wins.

'Booking all Tony McCoy's rides seems a long way from my boyhood days at Shepperton in Surrey where I lived with my parents bang next door to Kempton Park racecourse. I left school at sixteen and was like Tony in one respect, in that I took every opportunity to skive off from school to go racing. In those days children were let in free to racetracks, but had to be accompanied by an adult. I used to hang around outside until I saw some old lady, and then I'd latch on to her and get through the turnstiles with her. I was a 50p each-way punter, but I stopped gambling when I was eighteen, and it was the best thing I ever did. People imagine that running twelve of the country's top jump jockeys would provide a great chance to make money punting, but I make a good living through booking all the rides, and don't want to be tempted into spending my time backing horses. I have the trust of the leading trainers, and I would break that trust if I started punting.

'I was born on Champion Hurdle day in 1960, the day that Another Flash won. The Champion Hurdle has always been my favourite race, so Tony winning the 1997 Champion Hurdle on Make A Stand was a special thrill. As a birthday present every year I was taken to the race by my parents. I went to fourteen consecutive Champion Hurdles, but now I am far too busy and can only watch the race on TV. My first horse hero in racing was Monksfield, who won the Champion Hurdle in 1978 and 1979. My favourite jockey was Jonjo O'Neill. It's uncanny. I have no Irish blood in my body, but most of my heroes on the turf have been Irish, and nearly all my jockeys come from the Emerald Isle.

'I was desperately keen to get a job in racing, and luckily I got the job as racing manager to an Indian owner who had horses with Geoff Lewis at Epsom. Prior to that I had managed a pub at Walton-on-Thames. That was an Irish pub as well – I just can't seem to keep away from the Irish! We had quite a success with the Indian's horses, especially with a horse called Solo Style.'

Roberts then started acting as an agent and one day, out of the blue, Geoff Lewis asked him if he fancied booking the rides for his then jockey Jason Swift. Originally he started with a trial period of one month with Jason Swift, but it all clicked into place and he's been doing it ever since. Dean Gallagher approached him, and after that it was Richard Guest. Dave doesn't like flat racing at all, and he was very soon just working with jump jockeys. However, he says, 'If I did this job strictly for money, I'd pack up tomorrow. I soon realised that every time you book a jockey for a horse, you are putting his life at risk. Often I am contacted with offers to ride dodgy horses, but I watch every race on SIS and keep a list of the unreliable jumpers. There is no way I will accept a ride for one of my jockeys on a bad jumper. Over the years, and the more I do this job, the more I feel responsible for my jockeys. If I have any doubts, I just turn down trainers.

'I got wind through the grapevine that Tony McCoy was coming to England about two months before he actually joined Toby Balding, who had always been one of my closest contacts. I snapped him up the moment he arrived in England. I remember going to Plumpton on a Bank Holiday Monday in August 1994 to see Tony ride Omidjoy in a selling hurdle, one of the few meetings

I could get to. He was beaten six lengths by Adrian Maguire on Heretical Miss, but there was something about his riding that really caught my eye. I can be accused of liking people too easily but with Tony McCoy I struck up a real friendship, which is now based on great mutual respect. I knew from those very early days that I could recommend Tony to trainers who had never heard of him, in the safe knowledge that he would not let them down. From the first winner, Chickabiddy, it has all snowballed. Tony gives one hundred and ten per cent to all rides, and will agree to ride virtually anything.'

Roberts' mood changes dramatically as he recounts the blackest moment of his career as jumping's Mr Fixit: Friday, 19 July 1996 when one of his youngest jockeys, Richard Davis, died after a fall at Southwell. Roberts says, 'All my jockeys rang me that night and gave me a vote of confidence. I was completely shattered by Richard's death. At the end of it all, it was my responsibility that I booked the ride. No words can describe how I felt. I did give Richard the choice of whether to ride Mr Sox or not. To be fair, he had schooled the horse and was quite happy to take the ride. Richard was a very likeable young lad. He was not getting many rides, had to try his luck to get the breaks, and was happy enough to ride a few dodgy horses. I saw the race on TV and saw him fall at the very first fence. Later I was on my way to Durham to stay with my good friend, trainer Howard Johnson and his wife, when I heard the news of Richard's death on my car radio. I turned round and and came straight home.'

Dave Roberts really believes in British Telecom's maxim of 'It's good to talk'. On his desk are four different telephones, plus two mobile phones which are endlessly ringing. His yearly telephone bills reach over £8,000 and panic occurs when there is a telephone breakdown. Engineers are summoned very quickly.

When Dave organised his little jockeys' empire in Shepperton, he used to frequent a local William Hill betting shop to watch his team in action. These days he has SIS installed in his office, showing him all the races, but he often goes to the Ladbroke's shop in Redhill to watch races. If he ever appeared on TV's *What's My Line?* he would surely outwit the panel.

Roberts' big ambition now is to go through the card somewhere with six of his jockeys, for six different trainers – all as spare rides and not for the trainers they are usually associated with.

'What would be even better would be if Tony could go through the card himself and do a Frankie Dettori,' he says. 'It's quite possible as Martin Pipe is always seeking to go through the card himself, and one day he is certain to do it.' Dave's best day was 30 May 1994 when he booked his jockeys to ride seventeen winners up and down the country, including John Kavanagh to ride a winner on Nearco Bay at Uttoxeter, which was The Queen Mother's four hundredth winner. He has often provided all the jockeys in three or four-runner races.

People often don't believe Dave when he says that he has a strict no-betting rule, but there is no way he is going to give back to the bookies all the money he has earned.

'There's no point spending thirteen hours a day on the phone and slaving all morning, just to hand over the earnings to a bookie in the afternoon,' he says.

The secret of this game is that Dave finds out the entries as soon as possible and then rings round the trainers. The reason that as a freelance Tony rides so often for champion trainer Martin Pipe is that over eighty per cent of the time he has the horse with the best form in each race. Nobody can argue with that. The secret of Martin's success is obviously that he gets them superbly fit, but it's in his placing of the horses that he is so cute. He actually bothers to ring round and find out where his rivals' horses are likely to be declared. Because he is prepared to take the time to find out, he does not get many surprises when he sees the final declarations. Venetia Williams, who has made such a success of her training career from her Ross-on-Wye base, is another one who is not frightened to ring round other trainers to find out exactly what is running and where. Perhaps it is because she was an assistant to Martin Pipe for a while that she picked up a couple of his tricks.

Obviously Dave and Tony discuss all possible rides. Often Tony leaves the final decision to him, but they talk endlessly about the best choice.

'If there are two in a race, which Tony can ride,' Dave says, 'he rarely makes a mistake when opting for his choice of mount, and is ninety per cent right. He's got an uncanny level of success when his opinion comes into play. I remember after the 1996 King George VI Chase at Kempton, when One Man won easily with Tony falling at the last on Mr Mulligan, I phoned him in his car on the way home after racing. He was adamant: "One Man will never beat me again." He was dead right, as Mr Mulligan came out and won the 1997 Gold Cup, with One Man's Cheltenham jinx striking again as he trailed in a well-beaten sixth.

'My biggest task is to make sure that Tony keeps in one piece. If I put him on a poor jumper and he gets injured, we all suffer down the line and he has an obvious loss of wages. There is no flashiness in Tony. He might not smoke or drink, but he is still very much one of the lads. He is terribly down to earth. We have not had a cross word since day one. If I have sent him to one meeting for three losing rides, when he could have had a winning treble at the other meeting, he never moans. It's forgotten by the next day. If a trainer rings up and tries to book Tony for a horse saying, "The horse will need a run," I tell them to forget it. Tony McCoy is not riding any non-triers and everybody knows it. I can see him being champion for many years to come and I'm proud that I have been part of the action. As I tell people: I haven't missed a trick with this fella.'

Dave Roberts, such a vital cog in Tony McCoy's winning machine, has already had reason to thank his jockeys. In 1992 his son Josh, then four, had to have a rare leg-lengthening operation which could only be performed in Moscow. Wife Vicky stayed there for six months, as Josh, now fully recovered and an ardent Chelsea FC supporter, received his expensive treatment. It was Roberts' grateful jockeys who helped foot the bill. As Tony McCoy says, 'I know I speak for all his jockeys in saying that there is nothing that we would not do for Dave Roberts.'

CHAPTER 6

'It's a hard game, so it is'

Speeding around the country with Tony McCoy, travelling to and from the races, you soon become aware of his burning desire to ride winners. A long journey to some far-flung track to get beaten on two or three 'hot pots' is not the young Irishman's idea of a good day out, but in his exhausting profession there is always the next day's rides to look forward to. Even on the darkest winter's nights during the endless miles home, the mobile phone soon rings again; Dave Roberts wants to discuss future riding plans.

As his valet John Buckingham remarks, 'You very seldom see Tony McCoy flustered. He takes everything in his stride and overcomes any disappointments.'

In my experience I have never heard anybody utter a single bad word about the champion jockey. In a sport often riddled with petty jealousies, his close colleagues and rivals seem to enjoy sharing his moments of glory. To see him lifted aloft by his fellow jockeys at Stratford-on-Avon on the last day of the 1996–7 season was to witness a true show of genuine affection for A.P. McCoy.

Tony does not go out of his way to nick other jockeys' rides and he has a golden rule that 'I never take a ride from another jockey unless there is some very good reason – like the chance of riding the same horse in a future big race.'

Tony McCoy received a welcome addition to his 'team' for the new 1997–8 season when retired Admiral's son Nick Jackson became his driver. Previously Nick had been helping much-respected flat trainer Major Dick Hern.

Jackson soon realised the long hours McCoy spends in cars getting to race meetings. The first things to spot in Tony's car are a crumpled up copy of the day's Racing Post, and a pillow on the passenger's front seat so the non-stop jockey can grab a few minutes' sleep during a long journey. If people imagine that the champion jockey's life consists only of the enjoyment of returning to the winner's enclosure, they could not be more wrong.

C.D.

Records have come tumbling down like ninepins as I pursued an all-out attack on jump racing. In my first three seasons in England I have been lucky enough to be champion in each of the three campaigns. I had to have a laugh to myself when I read that my main rival, Richard Dunwoody – once my boyhood idol – was quoted as saying that I should take my foot off the throttle. That's a good 'un!

Richard Dunwoody is always on about the days he takes off. Then you read that on the two or three days he has gone missing in England, he has been riding winners galore in Ireland. I'll take it easy when 'Woody' does. Anyway, there will be plenty of time for slippers in front of the fire when I have retired.

As I roared towards the then quickest-ever 100 winners in a season in the autumn of 1997, Brough Scott wrote in the *Sunday Telegraph*:

> Watch Tony McCoy and wince. Never in jumping's long, thundering history has anyone galloped so fast towards the record books as this tall, lean, white-faced twenty-three-year-old from Moneyglass in Northern Ireland. And never have the fences looked so certain to get their man.

In an interview with Brough Scott at Cheltenham I had to agree that I'd suffered five really bone-crushing falls in the previous week; but I pointed out to him that these falls were the signal for you to 'kick on'. I pointed out that being the champion jump jockey is a hard game, so it is.

When I first started riding winners in England it was John Francome, a man whom I greatly respect, who took me aside and said: 'Get anything you can out of his game without having to go out there and actually ride in a race.' It was good advice, especially when you know of the terrible injuries – and, indeed, sometimes the death – of fellow jump jockeys. It's no picnic taking on those obstacles every half an hour, every afternoon of your life.

At this stage of my career I don't want even to think about how I am flying. That's the very moment when you have a nasty fall and make yourself look like a clown. Your luck can only last for so long, and I've been very lucky. People say that it is wrong to keep up my pace and that I will eventually burn myself out. I think a lot of people get more burned out thinking about what I'm doing than I do going through it. I can cope with feeling as burned out as this for the next ten years. There will be plenty of time for me to relax when I can't ride horses any longer; but tomorrow is another day, never mind ten years' time. If I can keep riding consistently for that length of time, I'll be the happiest man alive.

This game becomes obsessive. When you ride winners consistently, you want more and more every day. I hate it when I go racing for a day and don't have a winner. Maybe it was being so obsessive that got me here in the first place.

The 1996 Cheltenham Festival saw me open my account at the world's greatest jumping festival when the Philip Hobbs-trained Kibreet won the Grand Annual Challenge Cup at 7–1. It was a special feeling to ride into that number one spot for the first time, and I was delighted for Philip Hobbs, who had given me so many chances earlier in my career. I have been lucky in that the three jump trainers from Somerset (the Cider Mafia) – Martin Pipe, Paul Nicholls and Philip Hobbs – have supplied me with most of my flow of winners since I came to England. In the opening meeting at the Festival I was eleventh on Paul Nicholls' Call Equiname in the Citroën Supreme Novices' Hurdle, then I was unseated at the second fence on Paul's Captain Khedive in the Guinness Arkle Novices' Chase. In my first Champion Hurdle ride I finished tailed off last on Absalom's Lady, who was 66–1. A year later I was to finish at the other end of the race on Make A Stand. I was fourth on David Nicholson's Jack Tanner in the Sun Alliance Novices' Hurdle on the Wednesday and sixth on the Noel Meade invader from Ireland, The Latvian Lark, who was running in his first ever handicap in the Coral Cup. I was unseated four out on

Punters Overhead in the Sun Alliance Novices' Chase, so the meeting was not exactly a bundle of fun for me so far.

Everything changed on the Thursday, however. I started the day by being sixth on Zabadi for David Nicholson in the Daily Express Triumph Hurdle, and was seventh on Top Spin in the Bonus Print Stayers' Hurdle. Barton Bank gave me a super ride in the Gold Cup to finish fourth behind Imperial Call, ridden by my old friend Conor O'Dwyer, whom I had led into the winners' enclosure in Northern Ireland not so many years before, when I was a teenaged stablelad for Billy Rock.

Kibreet will always hold a special memory for me as my first Festival winner. I was lucky, rather like Mr Mulligan a year later in the Gold Cup, because I knew from quite a long way out that I was travelling on a winner. Kibreet was always going to win from the top of the hill because they had set such a good gallop. I had to give Kibreet a forceful ride but had four lengths to spare on the runner-up Easthorpe and jockey Jason Titley. Easthorpe was going for his seventh consecutive win of the season. I nosed into a definite lead three fences out and was never going to be caught.

It was a happy moment for Kibreet's part-owner Peter Emery. A year before he had Dr Leunt in the Triumph Hurdle, who was pushed out going to the third last and disqualified from second place. Emery and co-owner Terry Warner were, of course, thrilled, but Hobbs said, 'I thought that we had messed things up. Kibreet kept going up in the handicap after being placed in his last two races and I thought that he had too much weight. I also thought that the ground was too fast because he wants further than two miles. But Tony and I were lucky in that they went such a terrific early pace.' So, I left Cheltenham with my first Festival win under my belt.

Zabadi did not really enjoy all the hustle and bustle of the Triumph Hurdle at Cheltenham; but he loved Aintree and came home a very easy six-lengths winner for me in the Glenlivet Anniversary Novices' Hurdle. I was able to hold him and he quickened like a real star approaching the last, to run away from the runner-up Our Kris. Later that same day at Aintree I was able to win the Barton and Guester Handicap Hurdle on that old monkey Top Spin for John Jenkins. I really had to kid Top Spin into action, and we came from way back to get up on the line to pip Richard Dunwoody on Jathib by a neck. Top Spin was a 20–1 shot, and the on-course punter who had a cash bet of £10,000 to £500, must have been really chuffed, although he must have been more than slightly worried at halfway.

I had a lovely ride on Viking Flagship to win the 1996 Mumm Melling Chase for David Nicholson. At that stage of my career, before I had won the Cheltenham Gold Cup on Mr Mulligan, I was sure that this was the best chaser I had ridden, and over two miles and a half, that would still have to be the case. Viking Flagship was pure class that day as he defeated Sound Man by seven lengths in fabulous style. He has been a great servant to his owner Graham Roach, who produces over sixteen million rashers of bacon a year from his St Austell factory in Cornwall.

Amazingly, Viking Flagship had done plenty of running in his native Ireland, but had never got his nose in front in twenty-three races. He had a spell with Martin Pipe and won juvenile hurdles before he was snapped up by Graham Roach, who says proudly, 'I don't have to advertise my business. Viking Flagship does it for me. I even get good-luck cards for him, and one said, "You're there for Cornwall, my boy. Don't let us down."' Well, he certainly brought home the bacon when I won on him at Aintree.

I left Aintree in 1996 thrilled. In fact after my win on Viking Flagship Ray Gilpin reported in the *Racing Post*, 'Tony McCoy might have won the Lottery two weeks running judging from the way he was enthusing about the winner. McCoy beamed, "That was unbelievable. I will never have a better ride."'

David Nicholson was also thrilled, and said, 'That was the kind of performance you only see once in a very long time.'

My Aintree win on Viking Flagship won generous praise from the press. In the *Sporting Life* Alastair Down wrote:

There are some privileged people on this planet but few more than that lucky band who in the space of forty-eight hours have witnessed Cigar winning in the Gulf and that great warrior Viking Flagship strutting his stuff round Aintree. Yesterday Viking Flagship put his second place at Cheltenham behind him with a magnificent display which sent his jockey-for-the-day Tony McCoy into serious rapture. Not a waffler or dispenser of unjustified praise, McCoy simply said, 'I have never had a better ride.' Mind you, he didn't give the horse a bad one himself. Viking Flagship is tough and produces the best for his jockeys who are tough on him – a point amply illustrated by McCoy's comment: 'He wasn't travelling that well down the back, but the minute I grabbed hold of him he was like a different horse.'

Geoff Lester, the *Sporting Life*'s colourful race reporter, told his readers, 'Not since Kirk Douglas and Tony Curtis graced the film screens in the sixties has a Viking been more impressive!'

I really had high hopes that Paul Barber's Deep Bramble would win the 1996 Grand National. I had ridden him in his only previous race that season, when we had been fourth in a classy field for the Greenalls Grand National Trial at Haydock the previous February. He had been off the course for a long spell but jumped well and finished fourth behind Lo Stregone. We all knew that he would come on for that race, and he started at Aintree as a well-fancied 12–1 shot. He gave me a great feel through the race, but as he crossed the Melling Road for the second time we think that he must have ruptured his tendon and I was forced to pull him up before the second last. I am not saying that we were going to beat Rough Quest, who pipped Encore Un Peu after a tremendous tussle, but I am sure that we could have run into one of the minor placings ahead of Superior Finish and Sir Peter Lely. As I left Aintree after Deep Bramble's disappointment, I thought that I would be able to try again the next year, but due to my controversial 'unconscious' ban, I was not able to ride at the 1997 Aintree meeting.

Although I was receiving glowing reports in racing's two trade papers, the *Racing Post* and the *Sporting Life*, I did not realise that one or two sharp-eyed professional writers were beginning to take more than a casual interest in my progress. At around May time in 1995, most scribes' thoughts were on ante-post vouchers for the Derby and Oaks, with the big trials at Chester, York and Goodwood. George Ennor, however, much-respected senior race reporter of the *Racing Post*, was really beginning to take notice with a view to landing a good betting touch.

*　　　*　　　*

George Ennor recalls, 'It was not quite as dramatic as the conversion of Saul of Tarsus into Paul on the road to Damascus, but I can well remember the moment when it first occurred to me that Tony McCoy could be champion jump jockey. On Tuesday, 2 May 1995, at Ascot, I was covering an evening meeting of jumping for the *Post*. Tony McCoy had just won on Black Horse Lad in the Moonshine Novices' Chase for West Country trainer Jackie Retter. I have to say it was one of those seriously bad novice chases which the meeting seems without fail to provide.

'It was Tony's second winner of the evening. The first had been on Romany Creek for his mentor Toby Balding, a 20–1 shock in the Royal Fern Novices' Handicap Chase. After Tony's first win, high praise for the jockey was almost inevitable from the Weyhill wizard. That's not to say that it wasn't deserved, but it wasn't unexpected either. However, it was Mrs Retter's praise for Tony after he had won on her 11–2 shot that got me thinking. I was amazed how well Tony had got Black Horse Lad, an eleven-year-old novice, to jump and how he had done precisely what Jackie Retter had asked him to do. It occurred to me that if she was giving him rave reviews, other trainers would take the same view and snap up his services. The world could, as Arthur Daley once declared, be his lobster!

'The fact that he had ridden two winners that evening over fences was also part of my thinking. Back in the previous autumn Toby Balding had been talking about who might ride ex-Champion Hurdler Beech Road in the Mackeson Gold Cup at

Cheltenham. When McCoy's name was put to Balding, he had dismissed the idea virtually out of hand, saying that the jockey had had his first ride over fences in Ireland only a short time before. Yet here was the same young man winning novice chases over some of the stiffest fences in the country only a few months later, and doing it with the minimum of fuss. It really was the most remarkable progress.

'That very night on my drive home to Sussex, I decided to get my betting boots on. Other thoughts about the jump season and the championship suddenly fell into place. If McCoy was not going to be champion, then who was? Basically, you are down to only a very few runners in the race for the jump jockeys' crown. Many of them do not have the motivation to be champion when they really get down to it, and the hard fact is that most of them simply do not get the necessary number of rides. McCoy was different, but at that stage he was unconsidered and a real 'dark horse'.

'Much as I admire Adrian Maguire, I had to consider the realistic prospect of him being champion. He surely had his chance when he led Richard Dunwoody by 42 winners in January 1994, and was finally pipped 197–194. On that Ascot evening Maguire was nursing a broken arm from a fall at Hereford the previous month, and he just seemed to be injury prone. Unluckily for him, nothing has happened since to alter that impression, although Maguire remains a lovely character.

'At that time stories were going the racecourse rounds that the current champion Richard Dunwoody would not be renewing his association with Martin Pipe. Having achieved his championships, Dunwoody was keen to take a more relaxed role. The post as Martin Pipe's stable jockey almost guaranteed the title. Now I took on the role of Sherlock Holmes. Dunwoody, Maguire, Niven and Osborne were unlikely to win the title, but McCoy might. McCoy continued to ride winners through June 1995 and in the early days of July, but bookies still did not price him up in any lists for the jockeys' title. By the July flat meeting at Newmarket, I was ready to pounce – if I could get the decent price I wanted. The

William Hill Organisation were sponsoring the championship, and their David Hood was good enough to quote me 20–1. I dived in, though of course, you never have enough on.

'The first published price I saw for Tony McCoy being top jockey was 7–1, and as the season progressed I became increasingly and unbearably smug about jumping on the Real McCoy bandwagon. Even when I was told on the day of the Kingwell Hurdle at Wincanton that the Martin Pipe team had invested too much in their new stable jockey David Bridgwater for him not to be champion, I was not perturbed. My man, as I had almost come to regard A. P. McCoy, was still in front. Long before the end of the season, Hill's closed their book. It was all over bar the shouting and waiting for the postman to deliver.'

George Ennor and some of his press-room colleagues may have been dancing in the streets after Tony's first championship win, but it killed betting on the jump jockeys' title stone dead. David Hood of William Hill, an ex-jump jockey himself, says, 'We were not betting when Tony McCoy became conditional champion jockey in the 1994–5 season, and it was just as well that we were not. Tony turned the whole contest into a one-horse race – but then he has done exactly the same since with the senior jockeys' championship as well.

'I presented the conditional jockeys' title trophy to Tony McCoy at Stratford on the last day of the season on 3 June 1995, and within a short time George Ennor was asking me what price Tony would be to be the outright champion the next season. I thought that George had been at the cider! At that time it seemed an impossible task because of the dominance of Richard Dunwoody and Adrian Maguire. The jumping history books are littered with conditional jockey champions who floundered against the seniors when they lost their claims, and were never heard of again. When I did finally offer George 20–1 he nearly bit my hand off, closely followed by several other hungry hacks.

'That was the last season of William Hill's contract to sponsor the jockeys' championship. For the 1995–6 season the goalposts were moved with the introduction of summer racing and there was a further complication when Richard Dunwoody finally announced his split with Martin Pipe. We held off pricing up the championship until late July when Martin Pipe revealed that his new man was David Bridgwater. We opened the betting with 4–5 Adrian Maguire, 5–2 David Bridgwater, 11–2 Norman Williamson, 7–1 Tony McCoy, and 14–1 Richard Dunwoody. At this stage Tony McCoy had the cushion of a thirty-winner lead from summer racing, although there were still doubts about the amount of backing he would get from big stables and whether he would really be able to maintain his advantage. We thought that we were safe, as many of Tony's summer winners were for Martin Pipe, who in turn now had to use his stable jockey David Bridgwater. This was one runaway leader who never came back to his field, however . . . and cost us a bomb.

'By the beginning of November Adrian Maguire and Norman Williamson were ko'd by injury and McCoy was a sensational steamer as the winners kept rolling in. The tide was all against the bookies and there was no way of stopping it, although we still clung to the hope that the Martin Pipe magic would wear off on David Bridgwater. On 1 December we still bet 8–13 Bridgwater, 5–2 McCoy, 20–1 bar, but on that day the favourites flipflopped and for the very first time we made Tony favourite at 4–6, with evens Bridgwater, 20–1 bar. Finally on 24 March we waved the white flag of surrender – and took our boards down. McCoy had an unbeatable lead and was 5–1 on favourite. McCoy had done us. We don't often get things wrong. We would not be in business if we did. The press guys, who had a touch, were just the tip of the iceberg. Many professional punters also dived in, and took us to the cleaners. The stench of burnt fingers wafted over our Leeds head office for many a day and it was the worst result William Hill had ever faced in jockey championship markets. It was also the end of them. From then on the dominance of Tony McCoy has been such – like Frankie Dettori on the flat – that we simply have not played. But in fairness to us we were not just throwing a wobbly and picking up the ball to say that the game was over. So many times these jockeys' title races have been only two-runner affairs, and we have been crucified nearly every time.'

David Hood retired from being a jump jockey in 1990 after four years in the saddle. Spells with broadcasting led to him getting the press job with Hill's in 1992. He jokes, 'I rode thirty-five winners in four seasons after being with Stan Mellor, Nicky Henderson and Philip Hobbs. I was getting too bloody fat anyway and I managed to look beyond my blinkers and see there were more realistic ways of earning a living. I saw the light and quit. Thank God I did. Tony rode seventy-four winners in a season to be the conditional champion at the age of nineteen. I rode thirty-five winners in four years. My case rests!

'Bookies now suffer from the Tony McCoy and Frankie Dettori factor. Punters look at their rides and back their horses no matter what the form or the likely starting prices will be. If Tony McCoy ever went through the card at a Cheltenham Festival it would cost the industry millions. Of course, it's very unlikely, but now he is so obviously the best jump jockey that anything is possible. He has so much drive and dedication that he towers above the rest of the jockeys. I believe that he is seven pounds better than any jockey. He is so very powerful and strong, that he pulls races out of the fire to win, when he shouldn't be anywhere near the first three. We fear him more than a Tote monopoly!'

Tony McCoy had written his name in the record books by riding the fastest ever 50, when he scored on Rolling The Bones in the Brimfield Novices' Handicap Hurdle at Ludlow on Friday, 13 October 1995. This record was, of course, largely due to the advent of summer jumping. Later, on 17 January 1996 he reached his first century of winners when Amber Valley won the Bradmore Novices' Selling Hurdle at Nottingham. He reached his first 150 winners when Fools Errand won the Reynard Novices' Chase at Chepstow on 23 April 1996.

He was champion jockey for the 1995–6 season with 175 winners. His nearest rivals were David Bridgwater on 132 winners and Richard Dunwoody on 101. After he won the title officially on the last day of the season at Stratford-on-Avon, Peter

Scudamore penned in the *Daily Mail*, 'Tony McCoy's standard of riding this season has been superb, especially as it was felt by some that he lacked the experience over fences to trouble the more established riders for the title.'

CHAPTER 7

'I'd need a shrink if I was like Richard Dunwoody'

Tony McCoy is lavish in his praise for other jockeys, particularly his fellow Northern Irishman Richard Dunwoody. It's ironic that Woody was once McCoy's idol, as Jim Bolger's fresh-faced stable boy gazed into a television screen in a County Carlow betting shop. Now the two Irishmen clash head on daily, fighting out desperate jump finishes. Outright hero worship of Dunwoody may have changed to professional admiration, but there is no doubt that Tony finds Dunwoody's obsession with winning slighty too intense.

At the end of the long, strenuous 1996–7 campaign Tony curled up on a couch in his new Amesbury mansion and confided, 'Richard Dunwoody is the best – no question, but he is obsessed with winning, although maybe not quite as much as before he went to see his sporting shrink. The need to be first is his sole aim. He's a total professional and can be very intense. I probably am the closest to him in the weighing-room, but at the races he is really not on social terms.

'Away from the track, though, he tries to unwind and is completely different. You would not know that it was the same man. He came down to drive his racing car at Thruxton, and spent three or four hours afterwards at my house. He was laughing and joking and was a new man.'

McCoy and Dunwoody were doing the rounds of the hospitality boxes at Royal Ascot in 1997, when McCoy learned that

Dunwoody had recently had a couple of very unfortunate crashes on the motor-racing circuit.

McCoy posed the question to top-hatted racegoers: 'What is the difference between golfer Tiger Woods and Richard Dunwoody?' Beamed McCoy with the answer: 'Richard Dunwoody would like to drive 350 yards!'

McCoy gets on well with all his rival jockeys, and the way he was carried aloft by his fellow jockeys at Stratford-on-Avon on the last day of the 1996–7 season was a testimony to his obvious popularity. I know of only one incident – away from the races – when easygoing McCoy's temper reached boiling point. Tony's great friend Andrew Balding, son of royal trainer Ian Balding, was being hassled at a party by jump jockey Richard Guest. McCoy soon jumped into the fray, which did not really concern him, and Guest was decked as though he'd been chinned by one of Henry Cooper's famous sledgehammer left hooks.

McCoy has been a sensational knock-out in the saddle as well. He was the conditional jockeys' champion in only his first season in England and then grasped the full titles in 1995–6 and 1996–7. Not even the great artistry of Richard Dunwoody has halted the McCoy bandwagon.

C.D.

R ichard Dunwoody is in a world of his own – not as a jockey but as a person. Of course, he is a brilliant jockey, and in the 1996–7 season he topped a hundred winners for a record eighth successive season. However, he is in a world of his own in that he is very much obsessed by his riding and his desire for winners. I have been accused of being too keen on riding winners, but with Richard it is different, and I don't know when he actually switches off.

Richard was always my idol when I worked for Jim Bolger in County Carlow and watched jump races on TV in the lads' canteen, or nipped into Carlow to watch big races in the betting shop. It never crossed my mind that one day I would take over from Richard as champion jump jockey. I still rate him as the best jockey riding today, but I can never quite bring myself to call him by his nickname, 'the Prince'.

I have always thought that as a jockey Richard Dunwoody is superb. He has perfected the art of race riding, and when anybody congratulates me for taking his crown. I always reply, 'No, he gave it to me.'

Away from the weighing-room I get on with Richard really well. In fact, I am probably closer to him than any other jockey. I have had a good few laughs with him during evenings out on the town in London, but at the races he is deadly serious. All he cares about is winning the next race, and I admire him in a way for that. I've never had a row with him but there are certainly times after races when it is definitely not the moment to approach him; you can almost tell where he has finished by the look on his face. I, too, take it all seriously, but unlike Richard, once I come away from the track, I relax.

Richard went to top sports psychologist Peter Terry after the continuing problems with his race riding in 1994, and I'm not surprised that he needed to see a shrink, he was taking his sport so seriously. Peter Terry said at the time, 'Richard is so tense and wound up about life that I have given him a relaxation tape . . . and he's lost it!'

Richard produced a sensational comeback in 1994, and from January onwards wiped out Adrian Maguire's 42 winner lead to retain his championship title.

Now Richard is freelancing he seems slightly less intense, although winning is still the be-all and end-all to him, whether it's a little race at Newton Abbot or for a big prize at Sandown. He is one man you never want to see looming up at your shoulder in a hectic battle to the winning post.

On 2 December 1995 I was certain that I was about to ride the biggest winner at that stage of my career when I came to the last flight on Eskimo Nell in the William Hill Handicap Hurdle at

Sandown. Eskimo Nell was going for a four-timer in this competitive £35,000 handicap, and from two obstacles out I was sure that I was going to earn my biggest pay packet. However, Woody and I engaged in a tremendous tussle and he came and did me by a short head, although he did pick up a two-day ban for excessive use of the whip. Richard had a sensational day as he booted home a 225–1 four-timer, although I was able to break his stranglehold as I won the Doug Barrott Handicap Hurdle on Redeemyourself for trainer Josh Gifford. This meant a lot to the Findon trainer, as the race was named after his popular ex-jockey, who died as the result of a riding accident.

Michael Caulfield, secretary of the Jockeys' Association, probably summed it up best when he said, 'Dunwoody is so obsessed, whether it is riding horses, go-karts or motor-racing cars, that you wonder sometimes whether he is actually enjoying it.' However, Richard seems to smile a bit more now than when he was riding for Martin Pipe. The dark days when he clashed with Adrian Maguire and Luke Harvey – and was banned for the incidents – are thankfully all over.

One golden rule when dealing with Woody is not to try and get up his inner in a race. I never scream and shout during races, although some of my rivals never stop talking all the way round. I remember one day at Newton Abbot when I tried to make all on a horse on very soft ground. The plan failed miserably. My horse had stopped to almost a walk and I was fully two hurdles behind the leading group as they were about to finish. Suddenly I heard all this screaming and shouting behind me. There was a lot of clicking and slapping, and I wondered who was this lunatic jockey pushing the head off a horse obviously well beaten. I got the shock of my life when it turned out to be Richard Dunwoody, who yelled, 'I'll race you to the line.' I thought he really had gone mad. However, my horse had gone and Dunwoody won our private race. That made him smile, although you don't get too many smiles from him when the real battles are going on, or afterwards in the weighing-room.

My agent Dave Roberts is often in direct conflict with Richard Dunwoody's agent Robert Parsons. While Dave operates from Redhill in Surrey, Robert Parsons works from a town house in Kettering. The two have battled head on many times over the years, and never more than when Adrian Maguire – a Roberts man – was gunning for the jockeys' title with Dunwoody, only to lose 197–194.

Dave Roberts and Robert Parsons have never met, but when the declarations come out for the five-day stage at around 1.30 p.m. you can bet your life that a phone in Redhill will be lifted at the exact time one is being lifted in Kettering, and often the same number dialled. I like to think that Dave Roberts would be the first to try and book rides for me with trainers, but Robert Parsons is probably more ruthless. It is not nice to take other jockeys' rides, unless there is a good reason, but Parsons says, 'In the world of jockeys' agents, there aren't many rules. If we nick somebody else's rides, it's only because we are on first. If we do not take the ride, somebody else will. But, at the end of the day, we're only a voice on the phone for someone else. If Richard Dunwoody does not have a ride, he feels in a position to ride anything. It's that simple. I usually make the final decision what Richard will ride. Then I get rollocked if I get it wrong.'

Richard Dunwoody's great interest away from horses is Formula One motor racing. He is very friendly with David Coulthard, who gave him the splendid advice: 'Stay on the black stuff.'

Dunwoody admits, 'It's the adrenalin, the buzz, the competition. I'll retire in a few years' time from racing. You need something else, don't you?'

I have not the slightest doubt that Richard will always need a life full of competition. He admits, 'I was ruthless and obsessive when I was champion jockey. My number one priority was riding winners.'

In an interview with the *Daily Telegraph*'s Sue Mott, Richard Dunwoody revealed, 'I went to trainer Martin Pipe to be the champion jockey and it all went wrong because his horses caught a virus. Adrian Maguire was about forty winners clear of me by Christmas. Suddenly it started to get better and I nearly got to him before Christmas. Then, we were in a race when he was coming up on the inside. I thought that he was chancing his arm and pushed him off the course, out through the wings. I was totally in the wrong. I shouldn't have done it. I got banned for two weeks.

'The thing is that I was obsessive about winning, and it does tend to dehumanise you. Morning, noon and night, I'd be thinking about racing. In the end I went to Paul Terry, the sports psychologist, because I was so worried about Maguire that I couldn't concentrate on my own racing at all. Terry said, "Just control the controllable." It was common sense really. At that time, you'd tread on anybody's toes for a winner. Basically, there are no morals. But I am not as obsessive as I was. When I've done something, I don't look back. It's done. It's in the past. The only winners I worry about are in the future. I haven't got to the sad old state where I go back and watch my videos.'

CHAPTER 8

Martin Pipe – master trainer

God threw away the mould when Martin Pipe was born on 29 May 1945 at Wellington Maternity Hospital. He was to become far and away the most successful trainer in the history of National Hunt racing, but it is the way the bookmaker's son has revolutionised the sport which is so remarkable. He has created his winners' factory from Somerset without ever working for any other trainer, and became the champion trainer after originally learning about the profession from books. One can only have the greatest admiration for the way he has rewritten all the record books. He has not been known to court popularity and, in a very jealous sport, he has his enemies. However, some of his detractors are simply as green as grass with envy of his achievements.

Pipe has perfected the art of training. Under the tweed cap, or trilby, it is easy to spot Pipe's aggressive features at the races, with his prominent nose and the sharp, alert and piercing eyes. He always seems to be in a hurry and nearly every winner is greeted with his high-pitched: 'He did it nicely.' He is not at ease with strangers, or media men seeking information.

Thankfully, Pipe has recovered from the attack on him in 1991 by TV's Cook Report, which accused him of being an uncaring, commercial businessman with a huge turnover of often injured horses. To include Pipe in a series of programmes dealing with

drug barons, holiday timeshare spivs and vice racketeers was
simply scandalous. Quite simply, you don't train over two
hundred winners a year, which had never been done before, by
breaking down horses. The TV probe into Pipe's methods was
unjustified.

Seeking future running plans from Pipe can be a nightmare.
When I revealed in the Sun that he was splitting with Richard
Dunwoody, assistant Chester Barnes told the Morning Line,
'Don't believe all you read in the Beano.' Two weeks later
Pipe and Dunwoody announced that they were going their
own ways.

Pipe still loves a tilt at the bookies. I once asked Chester Barnes
why a millionaire trainer should need to bet. He replied, 'Martin
can't resist trying to put one over the bookies.'

The champion trainer is full of praise for Tony McCoy and says
simply, 'He is in a class of his own.' So is Pipe, although he did not
train his first winner until he was nearly thirty years old. Starting
with just one winner in the 1974–5 season, he trained only
nineteen winners in his first five seasons. Then the great win-
machine clicked into top gear, and the Pipe flow of winners has
seldom stopped for more than a single week.

It was all very different in those early days when Len Lungo was
Pipe's first jockey. Training thirty horses in the windswept hills
above Scotland's Solway Firth is a far cry from Nicholashayne for
Len Lungo, but the canny businessman, who also owns the Stag
public house in nearby Dumfries, well remembers his early days
with the unknown Somerset permit-trainer, who had not trained a
single winner.

Lungo recalls, 'In 1975 I was introduced to Martin Pipe. He
showed me his string of horses – just three of them. Two were so
fat that they had to be roughed off. That left us with Hit Parade,
and I rode him in a selling hurdle at Taunton on 4 December 1975.
In his previous runs Hit Parade had always belted his hurdles and
given away any chances of winning. So, long before racing started,
I walked round with Martin and loosened all eight hurdles to stop
them springing back, and made it easier for Hit Parade all the way

round. I remember loosening the hurdles as Martin screamed at me, "What are you doing? We'll all end up in jail." Hit Parade was backed from 2–1 to 5–6 favourite but made all to win by six lengths. Martin's bookmaker father Dave begged us not to go for a touch. He told us, "I intend to lay Hit Parade to any punters who want to back him with me. Mark my words – Martin Pipe will never train a winner."' Pipe Senior was proved wrong.

It was always on the cards that Pipe would spot Tony McCoy's great talents and seek to have him as his jockey. Their relationship is built on mutual admiration – two professionals at the very top of their trades – and there have been few disagreements between them. However, on one occasion Pipe wanted to put up a claiming jockey on a horse which had previously been ridden to victory by McCoy. The young Irishman pointed out with some force, 'If I don't ride that one . . . I shan't be riding the other three at the meeting for you.' Pipe relented and the all-conquering team marched on.

There was also the flare-up prior to the 1997 first day at the Cheltenham Festival, when McCoy overlooked his engagement with the Martin Pipe Racing Club. The old words 'you will never ride for me again' were used, but within two hours McCoy had won the Arkle Chase on Or Royal for Pipe. He then completed a glory day by winning the Champion Hurdle on Make A Stand. It was soon all sweetness and smiles.

Champion trainer Martin Pipe and his jockey counterpart Tony McCoy were destined to team up. Their joint love of winners is like a drug. It's the trainer–jockey partnership made in heaven . . . and hell for bookies.

For Tony's celebration party, organised by his management team RBI and held at Newbury racecourse at the end of the long, hard 1996–7 campaign, Hello! magazine, famous for its exclusive photo coverage, were part sponsors. Hello! has been the kiss of death for many engagements, marriages and big first nights, but as one wag said as he staggered off into the night at Newbury, 'It will take more than the dreaded Hello! magazine jinx to break up the Martin Pipe–Tony McCoy engagement. These two superstars were always meant for each other.'

Thanks to the advent of summer jumping, Tony McCoy was able to reach his best-ever score of 190 winners in the 1996–7 season. As he relaxes at his new Amesbury home he reflects, 'I was off for a total of two months with injuries and the odd ban for the old stick. My great ambition is to top 200 winners and go on to beat Peter Scudamore's best total of 221 winners in the 1988–9 season. Times have changed. John Francome's best score was 131 in 1983–4. Back in the late sixties and early seventies Bob Davies was champion three times, and in his best season he had a total of 91 winners.'

The staggering success of Tony McCoy can be judged by the fact that one bookmaker was even prepared to offer odds that one day the young Irishman would ride more than 259 winners in one season . . . more than Declan Murphy rode in his entire ten-year career in England. That's a measure of the McCoy magic. Backed by Martin Pipe's relentless will to win and his revolutionary methods, anything is possible for the most remarkable trainer and jockey combination the National Hunt game has ever known.

C.D.

There is no great mystique about Martin Pipe. Nine times out of ten his horses will gallop all the way to the line. Peter Scudamore was an ideal man to ride for Martin for all those title-winning years: Scu was very much blinkered on riding winners. However, Richard Dunwoody and David Bridgwater found the pressure too hot to handle.

David Bridgwater's decision to quit as first jockey to Martin Pipe might have surprised the outside racing world, but to those of us who witnessed the turmoil which seemed to be going through his mind daily, it was no real shock.

In a frank interview with Alan Lee of *The Times*, David Bridgwater said, 'In my last six months with Mr Pipe, I could have retired, just like that – packed up at the age of twenty-five. I had got so low you wouldn't believe it. I like to think I'm a jolly kind of bloke, but I just didn't enjoy what I was doing. I asked myself what the difference was, and there was only one thing – Martin Pipe. People tell me that I am crazy and that I could have been champion. I don't think about that – it doesn't interest me at all. I have never considered being champion. Is it worth putting yourself through all that? But none of this means that I am not ambitious.'

In a similar interview with the *Sporting Life*, he said, 'I could make up a load of bullshit, but let's just say that I didn't leave him lightly.

'People have asked me whether I regret my decision. They say things like, "Look at Pipe – he's just had another treble. You could have ridden them." Do they think I am stupid or what? As if I thought that Pipe was suddenly going to stop having winners or something? I thought it through all right. I went and spoke to a few other people, senior jockeys, and Peter Scudamore. I didn't just do it, but I didn't want to wait another twelve months, ride a bad race for Pipe, have a row, get the sack and then be left high and dry.

'Some of my bridges were being burnt. It's a fact that a lot of other trainers don't use Pipe's jockeys. It was different when Scu was riding – he was top dog and could get on and off, same as Richard Dunwoody – but I'm in a different category. I was having lots of winners and there was every chance that would continue, but while I was riding for Pipe, I was totally fed up with the game.'

David Bridgwater subsequently teamed up with colourful owner Darren Mercer, who shook the racing world when he took all his horses, including Banjo, away from Martin Pipe, and placed them with David Nicholson. The relationship between Bridgwater and Mercer was probably cemented at the 1996 Cheltenham Festival when two of the owner's best horses – Draborgie and Mack The Knife – were both killed. It was also a terrible blow to Martin Pipe, and he certainly did not deserve the cruel verbal abuse he received from the crowd. I know that Martin and his family felt so low that at one point he was even thinking of quitting, until close friends and owners persuaded him to carry on training.

I am sure that my experience with Jim Bolger in Ireland prepared me for riding horses which are at the centre of the betting public's attention simply because of the trainer associated with them. Jim Bolger is very competitive, and Martin Pipe is just as keen to turn out winner after winner.

Both Bolger and Pipe have the same way of conducting their business. It's interesting that both came from a non-racing-stable background, yet both have gone right to the top. Jim was an accountant at one stage, while Martin used to manage a holiday camp betting shop for his bookie father Dave Pipe. However, they both became champion trainers in their own field.

Bolger and Pipe would far rather be at home with their horses than out gallivanting around on racing's big social scene. After races they are both always in a hurry to get back to their stables, and you won't see them heading for the bar to have a celebration bottle of champagne with joyous owners.

People may say that Martin Pipe can be difficult, but I find him the easiest trainer of all to ride for. His horses always look very fit, and because they are tuned like athletes, they are the easiest horses to ride. If Martin tells me that a horse is fit enough to win, it is very seldom that I discover I am struggling in a race. Of course, it's no secret that Martin and his assistant Chester Barnes like a bet. Nobody likes losing, but if one of Martin's horses does get turned over, he has never blamed me. He is more likely to blame himself over some minor detail than to blame anybody else.

Despite all the intrigue which often surrounds the champion trainer, he is very uncomplicated when he comes to giving instructions. However, he does have one golden rule, and woe betide anybody who steps out of line on his strictest instruction: nobody, but nobody, is ever to reveal to the outside world how horses of his have gone on the gallops. He expects jockeys not to let on anything which has happened in his stables, and more important on his training gallops. Records have tumbled like ninepins ever since Pipe clicked into top gear, but within his relentless march forward is the golden rule that what goes on at home is secret. He would go bananas if he read in a newspaper that one particular horse of his was going exceptionally well on the gallops. I quite see his point of view and feel that other trainers would do well to keep the same veil of secrecy over their horses.

Martin Pipe is in a privileged position as his gallops are his own property, tucked away from the general public, and not open to daily scrutiny like the huge equine armies of trainers on Newmarket heath.

The gallops comprise a stretch of all-weather surface up a sharp hill in a field close to the Pond House stables. He worships that all-weather gallop and says, 'It's like a long carpet up the hillside but it places no strain on a horse's limbs.' His father Dave, an important part of the set-up, designed it all.

I have greatly enjoyed working with Martin Pipe, although it can be difficult, as he always waits till the last moment to declare his horses. Often I don't know where I will be going the next day until he has made his mind up where his horses will run, although this is a problem I can live with.

People pulled my leg when I moved from Weyhill to Amesbury, saying that I was moving nearer to Martin Pipe's stables on the Somerset–Devon border. Actually, I was only moving ten minutes nearer, and it still takes me one hour and twenty minutes to get down to Martin's stables for schooling sessions.

Many other trainers are simply jealous of Martin Pipe, and rumours about his methods often jump straight out of a Dick Francis thriller. However, I am sure that his success is due to the fact that his horses are worked to a peak of top fitness. If I ride for Martin Pipe in a race, it is usually because eight or nine times out of ten, his horses have the best chances of winning. You do not have to be a genius to want to keep in with a man with his tremendous record.

Martin's horses are highly tuned athletes, and nothing is left to chance. They are what I call hard fit. Some horses who have obviously been trained very hard, walk around looking like skeletons. They have been over-trained and have lost their strength through the hard work. Martin, however, has the knack of training horses to be a hundred per cent fit without losing any strength.

It's no secret that Martin has approached me to be his stable jockey. There has never been any retainer with the job, and Martin and his father Dave point out that they are capable of winning over £1 million a season in prize money, so the jockey's percentage is lucrative enough. It's a good argument: in the 1996–7 season I won 77 of my 190 winners for Martin Pipe, from a total of 219 rides. That meant that I won on thirty-five per cent of my rides for Martin, and more than one in three was a winner. My overall record of 190 wins from 664 rides meant that I was winning on twenty-nine per cent of my rides.

With Dave Roberts behind me I want to continue as a freelance for as long as I can. If I had been required to ride all Martin's horses I would not have won the Gold Cup on Mr Mulligan, and I might have been at Bangor or Stratford-on-Avon on 19 April 1997 and missed riding Belmont King in the Scottish Grand National.

However, you turn down a ride for Martin Pipe at your peril. I really put the cat amongst the pigeons when I decided to ride Cyborgo at Newton Abbot and not Flaked Oats for Paul Nicholls, but I knew I was teaming up with a potential Gold Cup runner for his debut over fences. It's worth remembering that Martin Pipe loves the little tracks for introducing his subsequent superstars. Both his 1994 Grand National winner Miinnehoma and top-class chaser Sabin du Loir started their careers as chasers at the Newton Abbot track.

Martin Pipe has achieved so much in his career. Up to 1997, of the big three races, only the Cheltenham Gold Cup has so far eluded his grasp. From the tiny Somerset hamlet of Nicholashayne he became the first trainer ever to turn out two hundred winners or more in a season. Back in 1990–91 he smashed yet another record when he became the first trainer to win more than £1 million in prize money in one campaign.

Martin is totally immersed in racing and once admitted, 'I'm afraid that I am rather boring. I don't think about anything else apart from racing. I even take the form-book to bed with me. But I do get a great thrill from winning. I don't like going to the races and losing.'

To see him cycling round his stables on his small bike is a great sight. Everything in his yard has been built from scratch. As his father Dave once said, 'Never tell Martin that he can't do something. He'll knock down a barn and build new stables in a day, if he puts his mind to it.'

Martin crams more work into his horses than other trainers, but in a given space of time, so that their nervous systems and limbs are not put under too much stress. His all-weather gallop is only six furlongs, and he works them over it with a pause in between. He makes sure that his horses do not have too much pressure on their lungs.

Martin shrugs when asked for his secret. He says, 'I try and remove all guesswork. The more facts and figures you have about your horses, the more you know. Weighing horses, having their blood tested all the time – all these things give you the scientific facts which you have to believe. I only deal in facts.'

Pipe has also made great strides in understanding the actual psychology of each of his horses – horses can become mulish and unhappy. He gets a lot of arthritic aches and pains himself, and is sure that learning how to cope with them has helped him to understand a horse's brain.

Many will say that the fact that Dave Pipe was able to sell his thirty-seven betting shops for more than a £1 million did not exactly hinder Martin's chances in life. The Pipe dynasty's wealth has been put at over £20 million and I'm sure that one day Martin's son David will take over.

Peter Scudamore hit the nail on the head when he told me, 'Martin Pipe has still got a bookmaker's brain. Everything has to be accountable. You don't make silly statements to him and there is no small talk. He listens to everything you say and it has to be right and accurate. It has to be fact. He's on top of everything and has got a very good, very orderly mathematical brain. Even after all his success, I feel that the operation is still improving. You can't get up early enough in the day to catch him out.'

I have no doubt that one day M. C. Pipe will go through the card at some race meeting, and I'm not so sure that it won't be one of the bigger meetings when everybody least expects it. We all recall Martin's great achievement in the 1992 Coral Welsh National, when he trained the first four home – Run For Free, Riverside Boy, Miinnehoma, and Bonanza Boy. A testimony to the Pipe procession is a framed copy of the *Sun*'s coverage of the race, hanging in his luxury lounge with the headline: 'UNFOUR-GETTABLE!'

Martin has taken jumping into a new dimension, although I suppose he will be very hard pushed to match Michael Dickinson's fantastic achievement in the 1983 Cheltenham Gold Cup, when he trained the first five home – Bregawn, Captain John, Wayward Lad, Silver Buck and Ashley House. I thought I was pretty clever when I won the 1997 Gold Cup on Mr Mulligan, but, unlike Graham Bradley on Bregawn, I didn't have a single stable companion to worry about.

Martin has tried to go through the card a few times at his local Newton Abbot, Exeter, and Taunton tracks. I've had three in a day at the big Punchestown Festival and the odd four-timer, but at Uttoxeter on 26 May 1997 I had my first five-timer, at odds of only 77–1 as they were all favourites. Martin Pipe provided me with three of the winners. I won on Glamanglitz (2–1), Strike-A-Pose (7–4), Doualago (2–1), Northern Starlight (5–4) and Nordic Breeze (2–5). I did not have a ride in the novices' chase, but Peter Henley did not arrive in time and Richard Lee snapped me up for Hangover. I had already won the first four races but Hangover could only finish fourth and so ended my race to beat Martin Pipe to go through the card.

A win on Martin Pipe's Indian Jockey at the evening meeting at Ascot on 25 April 1997, had its significance as it was the farewell appearance of the track's popular, closed-circuit-TV commentator Cloudesley Marsham, who kicked off his career with the mike back at Market Rasen in 1956. I had often heard his familiar Old Etonian tones echoing out over the loudspeakers. After I won the Tote Bookmakers Novices' Chase on Indian Jockey, which was his fifth win on the trot over fences, Marsham was kind enough to say, 'That was the riding performance of the season. Tony McCoy looked to be a sitting target for Mick Fitzgerald on Sublime Fellow, the 6–4 on favourite. McCoy seemed to be well beaten and had been niggling away at his horse virtually all the way round. He was off the bit from a long way out, made a bad mistake at the last. I thought Mick Fitzgerald was sure to win and was sitting there with a ton in hand, but Tony produced some real magic and won by one and three quarters of a length. It was a quite staggering performance. It was ironic that having covered over twenty thousand races, it was this win by McCoy on my very last night which will stick in my memory more than any other race. I was thrilled to see the genius in action.'

*   *   *

Alan Byrne, successful editor of the *Racing Post*, has a vast experience of watching races in his native Ireland and in England. At the end of the 1996–7 campaign Byrne said, 'I thought that Tony McCoy's win on the Martin Pipe-trained Doualago at Aintree on 16 May 1997 was probably the ride of the season. At the *Racing Post* we used to have the ride-of-the-season competition, and having watched this race from my office, I have no doubt that this should be the winner. Tony, of course, won far more important races than this £3,639 handicap chase on a Friday evening, but it was the way he took the contest which is such an abiding memory. From four fences out McCoy was having to chase Bas de Laine. Then he had to switch him and was all out on the flat to win by one and a quarter lengths. If you thought that this race would have sapped Tony's energy, you would be wrong. He came out later that evening and won on both Martin Pipe's Yubralee and Pond House.'

Martin Pipe was once quoted as saying, 'Tony McCoy is in a class of his own.' Champion trainer again after the 1996–7 season,

Pipe says, 'Tony McCoy is unbeatable in championships. He was conditional champion in his first season in England, when nobody had even heard of him. Then he was champion jockey in his first full season and then again champion in his third season in England. That's why I tell people that he is unbeatable. It's all in the record books. I have been associated with champions like Peter Scudamore and Richard Dunwoody – great men and great champions – but Tony has done so much in such a short time. He is exceptionally good. He has an old brain on young shoulders. After he won for me on Or Royal in the Arkle Chase and Make A Stand in the Champion Hurdle at Cheltenham in 1997 I was over the moon for him. He is a great jockey. But then he came out and won the Gold Cup on Mr Mulligan. I told him at the end of the meeting that he had completed a treble that would probably never be repeated.

'He showed his genius at Cheltenham on the first day. He was able to judge the pace so perfectly from the front on Make A Stand, and then come from behind to deliver Or Royal right on the line. Brilliant!

'I don't remember when he rode his first horse for me but Tony says it was Crosula, when he won at Uttoxeter in June 1995. I've looked it up and Tony made all in the handicap chase after making a few mistakes. That sounds about right!

'I have always known that Mr Balding has first claim on Tony, but I hope to use him as much as I can in the future. People still talk about that ride he gave my Doualago at Aintree in May 1997. Tony never gave up on the horse and kept responding to him. The jockey won the race – simple as that. It was quite exceptional and he kept Doualago jumping until he got him in front. That's typical of Tony. He tries a hundred and ten per cent on everything he rides, whether it is in a big race at Cheltenham, or a small one at one of the minor tracks.

'I admit that we did have one little mix-up at Cheltenham Festival before our double with Or Royal and Make A Stand. It was a misunderstanding and the only heated words ever between us.'

*   *   *

As I sat on the sidelines at my special celebration party at Newbury racecourse at the end of the 1996–7 campaign, I noticed that the most nimble performer on the dancefloor, with plenty of staying ability, was a certain Martin Pipe. When most of the jockeys had slumped off to the bar, the record-breaking trainer was still in full flight. Martin Pipe was leading them all a merry dance . . . just like most of his horses. Long may it continue.

CHAPTER 9

'You'll never ride for me again'

So little has gone wrong in Tony McCoy's sudden rise to fame that the smallest hitch is often greeted with great alarm. On 20 January 1997 the Racing Post announced the latest tremor in his roller-coaster career with a front-page lead proclaiming: 'McCoy in split with Nicholls'. The story concerned the fall-out between the champion jockey and Somerset trainer Paul Nicholls, over McCoy's decision to ride Martin Pipe's Cyborgo and not the Paul Nicholls-trained Flaked Oats in the small-time Bet With The Tote Novices' Chase at Newton Abbot that day. As a freelance McCoy obviously had the choice of all his rides, but Paul Barber, owner of Nicholls' yard and his main patron, was furious about McCoy snubbing Flaked Oats and said, 'McCoy won't ride for me again.'

Nicholls, who had enjoyed a good relationship with McCoy, was clearly the man caught in the middle of the row and said, 'I'm fairly flexible, but Tony and I have a gentleman's agreement that he will ride my horses, and he has broken that. My owners are giving me grief and I'm afraid that Tony will no longer have first choice on my horses.'

Owners and trainers have issued the 'you will never ride for me again' blast to jockeys ever since the days when Charles II rode up Newmarket's Rowley Mile on his way to meet his mistress Nell Gwyn.

Lester Piggott, despite his deafness, probably heard the immortal words more than any other jockey – and he was the best! The great Irish trainer Paddy Prendergast once stormed, 'I wouldn't employ Lester Piggott again for all the Crown jewels,' but within weeks he was putting up the Long Fella.

In 1978 Newmarket trainer Bill O'Gorman raged, 'Lester will never ride for me again,' after he had finished fourth on 15–8 favourite Abdu in the Champagne Stakes at Doncaster.

The most famous 'you'll never ride for me again' episode came when Piggott rode a filly for Ben Leigh, later Lord Leigh, in a race at Kempton in the seventies. Leigh relates, 'The filly was called Nigaire. It was the week before the Derby and there's no doubt that Lester was looking after himself. The saddle came off in the parade ring and the horse then trod on it. Lester was not keen to ride and persuaded the stewards that the filly was unsound. She was withdrawn and I was furious.'

There then followed the memorable spectacle of Leigh, even shorter than Piggott, dashing after him and wagging his finger in the great jockey's face as he yelled, 'You little twat. You will never ride for me again.'

Piggott just snarled, 'In that case I suppose I'd better pack the ****ing game in.'

Luckily, Tony McCoy was not forced into retirement by falling out with Paul Barber and Paul Nicholls. Quite soon he was back riding for the stable, and the unquestioned highlight of Nicholls' 1997 season was when McCoy won the Scottish Grand National on his Belmont King. However, the wounds with blunt-talking Paul Barber have not yet been healed, although Barber admits that 'never is a long time', and it's not a million to one that the young Irishman will soon be spotted wearing Barber's famous dark and light green colours.

Agents are obviously keen to get the best possible rides for their jockeys, and there are few rules in the jockey agents' jungle. It is the survival of the best. Top trainer David Elsworth, who has been very loyal to jockeys like Colin Brown and Paul Holley over the years, does not rate the agents' system.

'*They are all like dogs on heat when it comes to getting rides,*'
says Elsworth. '*Loyalty goes right out of the window.*'

*Happily, the vibes in deepest Somerset are that Tony McCoy
will one day reunite with Paul Barber, perhaps to fulfil the
owner's great dream of winning a Cheltenham Gold Cup.*

C.D.

Getting the sack for the first and only time in my life did hurt.
I was disappointed that Paul Barber took the action he did
over Cyborgo at Newton Abbot, because he didn't even own
Flaked Oats. The horse ran in the colours of Eric Swaffield, so to
this day I have never actually got off a horse of Paul Barber's to
ride one belonging to somebody else. However, I suppose people
thought that this would lead to the day when I would prefer to
ride Cyborgo rather than Barber's See More Business. I did not
want to upset anyone, and hoped I could keep all my various
trainers happy.

At that stage of the season there was a chance that Cyborgo,
who had shrugged off a twelve-month absence to win the Bonus
Print Stayers' Hurdle at Cheltenham in March 1996, could
become a Gold Cup candidate. He had schooled well for me
over fences and was already a Gold Cup entry. I didn't see how I
could be expected to pass him over for his debut over fences at
Newton Abbot to ride Flaked Oats, who was a promising horse
but had only won six of his eleven point-to-points. I had ridden
Flaked Oats for his debut over fences at Fontwell back in
December, where he ran on well to win by four lengths. The
connections were disappointed that I did not keep with him, but I
am sure at the end of the day they realised that Cyborgo had more
potential. After he won at Newton Abbot, he was 33–1 for the
Gold Cup.

I was on a hiding to nothing whichever way I went. I suppose
that Paul Barber and Paul Nicholls were worried that with David

Bridgwater gone, Martin Pipe was going to get a far tighter hold of me than they had, although they should have known that Dave Roberts is the only man with a tight hold of me. It was all very unfortunate, but people's stances can change. I very much hope that in the end I will get back in his colours.

Paul Nicholls is a former jump jockey and he started training at Paul Barber's Manor Farm at Ditcheat, near Shepton Mallet in Somerset, in 1991. Paul rode 118 winners in his career from 1981 to 1989, including the Hennessy Gold Cup on Broadheath and Playschool in 1986 and 1987. Paul is six foot tall and weighs a healthy fourteen stone these days, a far cry from when he tipped the scales at 10st 7lb.

Like myself, for Paul a broken leg was the turning point in his career. My broken leg saw me switch from flat to jump riding, but in Paul's case, the injury ended his career.

*			*			*

Paul Nicholls readily admits, 'Breaking a leg was the best thing that ever happened to me. Every summer at the end of the jump season my weight used to shoot up from 10st 7lb to 12st 7lb and every year I was virtually having to starve myself down to get ready for the new jump season. I was getting fed up with practically living in a sauna to lose two stone every season. When I had the break I remember lying in agony in a hedge, waiting for the ambulance, and thinking, thank God, now at last I'll be able to tuck into a decent meal.

'It was after Jim Old left the Manor Farm stables that Paul Barber advertised for a new trainer. I only had ten horses to fill forty boxes, but Paul was good enough to give me a try. Our first winner was Olveston, who was part-owned by my policeman father, when he won at Hereford on 20 December 1991.

'If you had seen Tony on my schooling ground you would never have doubted for one second that he was going to be champion and probably for many years to come. I reckon that it's when you see jockeys riding schooling work that you appreciate whether they have got it or not.

'I am often asked which of Tony's many wins for me has been the best. I select Belmont King in the 1997 Scottish Grand National because I feel that his genius stole a big race. But if I had to name one race where Tony's ability was seen at its most effective I would have to pick his win on Bramblehill Buck that enjoyable day at Newton Abbot in December 1995 when I had my first treble at one track. Okay, it was only a £2,872 handicap chase but Tony was unreal in that contest. I am convinced that no jockey, who has ever sat in a saddle, would have won on that horse that day . . . apart from Tony McCoy. The horse was one of the slowest on earth and looked cooked at the last fence but still went on to win by five lengths. Tony was "at" the horse from the word go, and from over two and a half miles urged my horse to victory. He made the horse win – simple as that. It was funny that he won on my James The First the same day. He was the biggest monkey ever to run in a race, and for Tony to win on both these horses in one afternoon was the eighth wonder of the world.'

*   *   *

My relationship with Paul Nicholls turned horribly sour after the Cyborgo–Flaked Oats affair, but Paul and I never really fell out ourselves, and I am sure that I will ride many more winners for him in the future.

My first ride for Paul Nicholls had been on Warfield in the Philip Barnard Memorial Conditional Jockeys' Handicap Hurdle at Sandown on 17 February 1995. I tried to make virtually all that day but was collared by Jadidh and finished second, beaten by three lengths. It was quite a while after that race that I teamed up with Paul again.

*   *   *

Paul Nicholls remembers his first booking of Tony well. At the close of the 1996–7 season Nicholls said, 'I had seen A. P. McCoy riding in the West Country ever since he arrived from Ireland and was very impressed. I could see that he was a natural rider and that his attitude was first-class. I booked him up for that boys'

race at Sandown and hoped that he'd make a dream debut for me.
He nearly did! I can remember driving home in the car afterwards
with my wife Bridget and we both agreed that Tony had exceptional talents, even at that early stage of his career. We thought
that he would be a handy chap to have riding for us the following
season on a full-time basis, but Tony was still with Toby Balding
and we came to an arrangement that Toby and I would share his
services. I was lucky that season in that Toby had a quiet time and
Tony rode more winners for me than anybody else.

'He regularly came down to school my horses and I was very
impressed with his work. At that stage of his career he had not
ridden many chase winners. He looked terrific over hurdles
but, with lack of experience, he had still not mastered the full
art of riding over fences in races. Some of my friends thought
that I was mad to let him school my horses over fences. At that
time I had novice chasers coming out of virtually every stable
door. I was swamped with them. Tony took on the task of
schooling them over the bigger obstacles and there was no
better man. He was superb. I could almost see Richard
Dunwoody in him as he popped these novices over their first
fences at home. He has a natural gift. When he gets to the races
he has such a great desire to win that his combination of talent
and ambition are unmatchable.'

*   *   *

Paul Nicholls has been on an upward curve ever since he started
training. In his first season he saddled 10 winners, and since then
his end-of-season scores have been 29, 28, 53 and finally 56 in
1996–7, worth £359,318, when the highlight was my victory for
him on Belmont King in the Scottish Grand National. The score of
56 and the prize money put him seventh in the trainers' list.

Paul was assistant to his former boss David Barons when the
Devon trainer won the 1991 Grand National with Seagram. He
has often shown me one of Seagram's racing plates at his stables,
and admits, 'I look at that racing plate every day of my life and
think how nice it would be to have another for a horse of my

own.' Deep Bramble looked every inch a Grand National horse in 1996, but sadly I had to pull him up lame before two fences out.

Paul says of his training techniques, 'Since I started training I suppose I have moulded myself on Martin Pipe and Nigel Twiston-Davies, both of whom concentrate on getting their horses really fit at home. If horses are fit they are less likely to damage themselves on a racecourse. When I was riding, there were some trainers who knew in advance their horses wouldn't be fit until they had enjoyed three runs. That is unacceptable these days.'

I was united with Paul Nicholls for a red-letter day at Newton Abbot on 11 December 1995 when I rode his first-ever treble at one track on Court Melody, James The First and Bramblehill Buck. This was a 103–1 treble and put the score in the battle for the jockeys' title on 88–68 in my favour against David Bridgwater. The *Sporting Life*'s Steve Taylor was spot on when he reported, 'Tony McCoy is a very hard man to pass at the moment.' I also won a few admirers at Plumpton on 13 November 1995 when getting Walking Tall home in a novices' hurdle. Trainer Tom McGovern was kind enough to say, 'Tony gave him a great ride – he's brilliant, the boy, isn't he?'

When Cyborgo won at Newton Abbot I really didn't know which way to look. I realised that I had openly upset people who had been magnificent to me before. In my column in the *Sun* I wrote:

Cyborgo's winning chasing debut at Newton Abbot was not the happiest moment of my life, but I was mighty relieved. It was a very sad day for me when trainer Paul Nicholls and I split over my decision to ride Cyborgo for Martin Pipe instead of Paul's Flaked Oats, who fell. I told Paul on Sunday that I would ride Cyborgo, and he replied that if I rode that horse it was the end of our partnership, which was based on a gentleman's agreement. Paul has been very good to me since I came over from Ireland and it was not a decision that I wanted to make. I hope that I can ride for Paul in the very near future, although I have a feeling that when you fall out with some of his owners, you stay fallen out. It would be a sad day if I couldn't get back on horses like See More Business and Belmont King. I hoped that they would be potential Gold Cup and Grand National winners.

Now I will ride as freelance until the end of the season, and then have a rethink. In the end I suppose it was inevitable that one day I would have to make a firm decision and upset one party or another. I am very sorry that it has happened, and will just have to carry on as best I can. Paul Nicholls has some lovely horses and we had some great moments, but he wanted more commitment from me than I was prepared to give, and I am afraid my decision to partner Cyborgo was the breaking point. I have schooled Cyborgo several times and know his potential. He could be a Gold Cup winner and Martin Pipe has always thought the world of him. Martin has been kind enough to say that I am in a class of my own, and there is no better trainer than Martin at getting horses to the Festival – a point he proved when Cyborgo won the Stayers' Hurdle last season first time out. I never wanted to upset anyone, but I suppose that I am gambling on Martin Pipe doing the same trick at this year's Festival. As the saying goes, as one door closes, another one opens.

I was told that I was becoming like Lester Piggott in his heyday as a freelance jockey on the flat: all the top trainers wanted him, and he never minded trying to get on the very best ride in every race, often chopping and changing with little regard for owners he had previously ridden and won for. Lester Piggott was so good that he usually got away with it.

*   *   *

Before the start of the 1997–8 season Paul Barber was still adamant. He said, 'You will not see Tony McCoy riding in my colours. I said that he will never ride for me again, and never is a long time! Tony was wrong to accept the ride on Flaked Oats and then be pressurised by Martin Pipe. I'm a bit old-fashioned, and if I say something, I stick to it. However, I must stress that I have nothing against Tony McCoy – he's a good lad. It is what went on behind the scenes which made me mad, and agents sometimes need a left hook on the jaw! I have made up my mind, although maybe my idea of never is for at least a year anyway. Perhaps next January we will decide that Tony's spell in the wilderness for us is over. Tony McCoy is without doubt the finest jump jockey riding today. He can do without us ten times more easily that we can do without him. I'm not naive and I accept that he is the best. I'm not so bitter and twisted not to realise his great ability.

'I knew the moment that David Bridgwater split with Martin Pipe there would be trouble regarding the availability of Tony. I have no doubt that Tony can ride all the Pipe horses to his satisfaction, but I question whether he can stand the mental pressure, and if the job with Pipe were full-time for Tony, I believe it would drive him crackers. Don't forget that Richard Dunwoody and David Bridgwater did not last all that long.

'I have the greatest respect for Martin Pipe. I have known him for years and he is quite entitled to play the game his way, as he often holds all the best cards. After the row over Cyborgo and Flaked Oats at Newton Abbot, Pipe came over and said, "I am sorry all this happened. I never would have put up Tony if I had known that it was going to cause all this trouble."

'I have no animosity towards Tony McCoy. I was just very disappointed that he had broken a gentleman's agreement. As far as I'm concerned, a handshake is as good as a written contract. I can't possibly put up Tony on one of mine again, and my partner John Keighley agrees with me, although I do admit – never is a long time.'

Paul Barber has been an owner for over twenty-five years and makes no secret of his big ambition. It is well known amongst his friends that he has two ambitions in life – to milk a thousand cows and win the Cheltenham Gold Cup. He achieved the first one after fifteen years, and is determined to have a good attempt at the other.

'The only trouble is that I am fast running out of the cash necessary ever to own a horse to win the Gold Cup,' he admits.

It was Barber's sporting uncle who introduced him to the world of horse racing via his good horse Simon de Montfort. A hunting man, Paul Barber became a very successful dairy farmer, and his great desire to milk a thousand cows was achieved with far more speed than his Gold Cup ambitions.

                              *   *   *

Even before I was born, Paul Barber was a well-known figure on the West Country racing circuit. His light and dark green silks with the white 'V' sent many a Somerset racegoer home happy after wins on horses trained by popular John Thorne. After John Thorne's tragic death, Jim Old was Paul Barber's trainer before Paul Nicholls became the master of Manor Farm stables on the 2,500-acre farm at Ditcheat, near Shepton Mallet in Somerset.

In those days the most popular horses to run in the Barber colours were the outstanding chaser Artifice, and Arctic Beau.

Gazing out at a rolling Somerset paddock Mr Barber is lucky enough to see his one-time pride and joy Artifice, winner of twenty-one races, still enjoying life at twenty-six years of age. He says, 'Artifice is creaking a little bit, but he is still leader and in charge of the pack. He's enjoying life.'

It was Artifice who gave Mr Barber the greatest thrill of his life when he won the Black and White Whisky Gold Cup at Ascot.

However, I know that Paul was on a high after I won the Crowngap Winter Novices' Hurdle on his See More Business at Sandown on 1 December 1995. He won by fifteen lengths under me that day and I've never ridden an easier winner. I cruised into the lead two hurdles out and beat Father Sky as easily as I liked.

Chaseform were kind enough to note that See More Business 'stormed clear with the minimum of fuss to win doing hand-springs. He will now have a break before returning for the £20,000 Premier Auction Novices' Hurdle at Wincanton in February, for which he must have an outstanding chance, followed by the Sun Alliance at the Cheltenham Festival. He looks a seriously good novice.'

I had never ridden a more certain pre-Cheltenham winner, and I recall that after the Sandown race John Francome pressed Paul Nicholls to take the bull by the horns and run See More Business not in the Sun Alliance but in the Champion Hurdle. I have to say that at that stage I would rather have been on See More Business than my ultimate Champion Hurdle ride Absalom's Lady, who was last of the fourteen finishers at 66–1 behind Collier Bay.

I very much hope that this squabble will be sorted out quickly. I would also love to end a jinx, as neither Paul Barber nor Paul Nicholls has yet had a winner at the Cheltenham Festival. Riding a winner for them there would surely put me back in their good books.

If I have to serve a one-year sentence, so be it, but I'm rather hoping that after Belmont King's win in the 1997 Scottish Grand National, I will get a quick remission for good behaviour!

CHAPTER 10

'Make A Stand can deliver'

The two sides of Tony McCoy's unique talents were ably demonstrated when Or Royal came with a grinding late challenge to overhaul Squire Silk in the Arkle Chase on the Cheltenham Festival's first day, followed later by Tony setting off in front like a scalded cat on Make A Stand, when he was never headed, to win the Champion Hurdle. The media who thronged round champion trainer Martin Pipe in the winners' enclosure to greet Tony McCoy and both the winners from the Nicholashayne maestro, could hardly have guessed the tension which had preceded the first day of the world's greatest jumping festival, when the successful trainer–jockey partnership nearly cracked.

McCoy's management team had signed a deal with Guinness incorporating the sponsorship of Mr Mulligan for the Tote Cheltenham Gold Cup. Part of the deal was that the champion jockey would visit the Guinness hospitality boxes to give a short talk before racing. As usual, traffic into the great jumping amphitheatre was snarled up by thousands of cars all heading to the same spot in the Cotswolds. Many of the Guinness guests were late, and McCoy, anxious about this most important single day's racing of his career so far, was kept waiting. Minutes ticked away before he was able to give racegoers his informed talk about the day's racing and the obvious chances he felt lay ahead for Or Royal and Make A Stand.

However, while he nattered rather nervously away to the Guinness clients, he clean forgot another engagement. He was also due to address the Martin Pipe Racing Club in their private tent. The appointed time went by, and McCoy failed to appear, much to the annoyance of Pipe.

When McCoy finally made his way back to the weighing-room he was greeted by a verbal barrage from the furious Pipe.

The famous 'you'll never ride for me again' line was used, although happily the situation soon changed, when Or Royal and Make A Stand came back to thunderous ovations.

'Didn't Tony McCoy give them a brilliant ride?' Pipe was heard to ask reporters, as usual his eyes darting from side to side as though he is never quite sure whom he wishes to address.

Looking back at the great day and the unknown pre-race tension, McCoys says, 'It was terrible. I was held up in the Guinness tented area and completely forgot about the Martin Pipe Racing Club, who were all waiting for me. Martin Pipe sent out search parties looking for me, but it was impossible with all those crowds. I should have been with his people – no question. I let him down badly, and he is naturally always very keen to please his club members. He was fully entitled to be very angry, and he gave me the verbals all right. However I was not at Cheltenham to be talking in everybody's box: I was there to ride winners, and I rather feel that I made up for it by winning the two major races that day on M. C. Pipe's Or Royal and Make A Stand. If I had got beaten on them both, though, my name would really have been mud.'

C.D.

'**M**AKE A STAND CAN DELIVER', screamed the *Sun*'s front-page headline of their four-page Cheltenham pull-out. The old 'Currant Bun' can't be accused of doing things by half! 'I'll make it in the Champion', roared the second deck of the headlines, and I wasn't wrong. For my *Sun* column that day I wrote:

Stand by! I'm out to make every post a winning post to win this afternoon's Smurfit Champion Hurdle. Martin Pipe's Make A Stand gives me a fantastic chance of a first win in the race, and my plan is simple: I am going to run the others off their feet. Night Nurse in 1976 was the last hurdler to win the Champion from the front and I'm confident that Make A Stand will never be headed.

Make A Stand has won his last four races, so he is on a terrific roll. He keeps improving and has shot up by nearly two stone in the ratings this season alone. What's more, the dry spell will help him. The fast ground will not suit several of the other fancied runners, one of whom is the current title-holder Collier Bay. I greatly respect him, but it cannot be in his favour that he has only run once this season.

Martin Pipe, who won the Champion Hurdle with Granville Again in 1993, is usually supremely confident, but says that there is no way that Make A Stand can reverse his fifth behind Space Trucker here at Cheltenham in November. However, I believe that race was set up for Space Trucker . . . and Make A Stand has improved hand over fist since then. Just look at his form. I rode him when he spreadeagled his rivals in the Sun Lanzarote Hurdle at Kempton in January, and he was even more impressive in the Tote Gold Trophy at Newbury in February when Chris Maude anni- hilated the opposition to win by nine lengths. If he handles all Cheltenham's ups and downs, he will take all the beating. That's my one fear: Make A Stand is such a fast hurdler, but all his best form has been shown on flat tracks.

Writing on the eve of the world's greatest jumping festival, Marcus Armytage, who won the 1990 Grand National on Mr Frisk, summed up the atmosphere nicely when writing in the *Daily Telegraph*: 'Cheltenham was shrouded in mist yesterday morning, a dust sheet over jump racing's most precious furniture.'

However, the whole sport was under a cloud, for at the South-east Hunts Club point-to-point at Charing, Kent, the previous Saturday, Giles Hopper, an apprentice farrier, died after a fall. Hopper's death, after being thrown from The Mill Height at the second fence, highlighted again the dangers jump jockeys encounter. Hopper, who was only twenty-one, was the fifth point-to-point rider to die in a race since 1980, and the ninth fatality at the time in all forms of racing in the past twelve years.

My heart also went out to Adrian Maguire, one of my closest friends in the weighing-room, who was cruelly forced to miss Cheltenham for the third year running. Adrian missed the entire 1995 Cheltenham Festival because of the sudden death of his mother, then in 1996 he was sidelined with a broken collarbone. His hoodoo sequence continued in 1997 when he broke his right arm in a fall at Leicester on 25 February. I had plenty on my mind when I walked out to ride Make A Stand.

The Champion Hurdle race itself went like a dream for me. When I gave Make A Stand a breather at the top of the hill, I glanced round at the opposition. I couldn't believe how well I was going and could see that the rest of the field were already under pressure. Believe me, this Make A Stand is some hurdler. I suppose punters will look back and think that he must have been the biggest certainty of all time when he was running in those handicaps earlier.

Make A Stand's task was made easier by the curious display of Large Action, who was backed down to 7–2 favourite but was pulled up by Jamie Osborne after jumping only the second hurdle. The reigning champion Collier Bay also disappointed and was pulled up by Graham Bradley before three hurdles out. In the end it was Theatreworld from Ireland who finished second, with Space Trucker third. One of my favourite photographs is a shot of Make A Stand jumping the last with the rest of the field out of it.

Jim McGrath wrote in the *Daily Telegraph*:

Tony McCoy consolidated his position as the new hero of the weighing-room with a super ride that landed him, owner Peter Deal and trainer Martin Pipe yesterday's Smurfit Champion Hurdle with the bold-galloping Make A Stand. The gelding set a course record in winning by five lengths. For a horse whose connection with National Hunt racing began, curiously enough, by winning a Leicester claimer on the flat two years ago, Make A Stand has made staggering progress, and he put his quick-jumping technique to devastating effect to make virtually all.

With speed to burn between each of the eight flights, and relishing the ground that was undoubtedly faster than the official 'good', Make A Stand ran his rivals ragged to the home bend and then held on gamely up the notorious Cheltenham hill. McCoy's judgement in front on Make A Stand was masterly. He allowed the gelding to bowl along after jumping the third flight, thus opening up a gap of ten lengths on the field, but gave him a breather at the top of the hill before allowing him to stride down it.

Martin Pipe was a happy man afterwards, but in his club members' tent I understand he was seen watching the race on TV, and as we came to the run-in he shouted, 'He's beat, he's beat. He'll stop.' Martin had been worried that the watered ground might stop Make A Stand, but he should have known better.

Wise old Peter Easterby watched it all with a typical knowing Yorkshire smile. The man who trained five Champion Hurdle winners, including front-running Night Nurse, said simply, 'To think that we tried to beat Make A Stand in a handicap. Now we know why we couldn't!'

Early on in the season I knew that Martin Pipe thought a lot of Make A Stand. He'd been claimed, as we all know, for just £8,000, which must go down as the bargain of the century. There was no way Martin got that horse to run on the flat – he sees everything that moves on a racecourse as a prospective hurdler. I won on Make A Stand at Ascot and Kempton, making all both times. There was talk of him going for the Supreme Novices' Hurdle and not the Champion Hurdle, but I was pretty sure that M. C. Pipe would not let the big one slip away.

At Ascot, when I rode him for the first time, it was the old story, and the form boys noted, 'Jumped well, made all, well clear after the third, won unchallenged.' His win in the Sun Lanzarote Hurdle at Kempton was surrounded by all the fuss of Martin Pipe double declaring Pridwell, which under the then rules, he was quite entitled to do. The way Make A Stand scooted round

Kempton that day it would have taken an earthquake to stop him. I was invited into the *Sun*'s private box afterwards, and Rob Hartnett, then of Coral's, handed out his ante-post list for the Champion Hurdle. Coral's still went 40–1 and I remember telling Martin Pipe's eager son David that those odds were far too long. Master Pipe got the message!

Make A Stand is without question the best hurdler I have ever ridden, and I have a sneaking feeling that I may never ride a better one. He's like a coiled spring waiting to explode. I've never ridden, or seen, a horse who hurdles so naturally. He seems to flow over the obstacles. What people forget is that he won the Champion Hurdle as a six-year-old and still a novice. I am certain – barring accidents – he will win more Champion Hurdles, and he can only get better. He won the William Hill Hurdle at Sandown, the Sun Lanzarote, the Tote Gold Trophy and the Champion Hurdle all the hard way – from out in front. I have never been beaten and virtually never headed on him, and I'd like to think that it stays that way!

When he got beaten next time out, at the Grand National meet in the Martell Aintree Hurdle on 5 April 1997, I was supposedly suffering from concussion and was not allowed to ride. Unlike in all his other races, Make A Stand and Chris Maude were not able to get away from the rest of the field. I am certain that Make A Stand was tired after a long season. Before the race he looked fine, but inside he must have had enough. For the first time that season he was challenged from both sides, and turning into the straight it was clear to me, watching on TV at the track, that he was not going to win. Bimsey, who likes Aintree, won again, with Pridwell in second. The fact that the Champion Hurdler started at 7–4 against told its own story. Some claimed that Make A Stand finished lame, but he seems fine now and a new campaign awaits this very exciting horse. He has such a high cruising speed and he's like a Rolls-Royce. You can put him where you want to at any stage.

Make A Stand's Champion Hurdle victory was a fairytale come true for his main owner Peter Deal, who really deserved to hit the jackpot after several stories of bad luck and broken dreams with previous horses. Mr Deal, who was born in Cheshire but now lives in Wiltshire and London, has always been a sports fanatic, with special interests in cricket and racing.

Peter Deal takes up the story of how Make A Stand, a modest horse on the flat with at one stage only three wins from sixteen races on the level, became the fastest-ever winner of the Champion Hurdle.

*   *   *

'I registered my colours of dark blue and yellow back in 1973 but I have had so much bad luck that at one stage I was very seriously thinking of changing them. I've had promising horses who have been killed. One of my best broke his neck in a race. Many years ago another of my tip-top horses was the very promising hurdler-chaser Fort Belvedere, who had a brilliant first season as a novice. However, at Ascot he broke down very badly. We gave him plenty of time and patched him up and he duly won his first novice chase very easily, but he was never the same again.

'I suppose I was due a change of luck and it came along in the shape of Make A Stand.

'I spotted him at Wantage trainer Henry Candy's as a yearling. I have had horses with Henry for a long time. I can remember thinking what a remarkable resemblance the young horse had to his sire Master Willie, who was a favourite horse of mine. We formed a syndicate and that's how the fairytale unfolded.'

*   *   *

Make A Stand ran five times as a two-year-old in 1993. His first-ever race was at Sandown on 11 June when Billy Newnes rode him over seven furlongs. He started 20–1 that day and finished fifth of the ten runners. The winner of the race was Paul Kelleway-trained Venta de Possa, who was ridden by Frankie Dettori. *Raceform* described Make A Stand as 'leggy, with scope'. He later ran at Newbury, Haydock and Ripon and rounded off his first season by winning the Fen Ditton Nursery at Newmarket, when Billy

Newnes got him up by a head to win a twenty-three runner race. These races are not easy to win.

As a three-year-old he had just the one race at Bath on 26 April when he finished eighth of ten. The combination of a subsequent virus and being gelded meant that he was a sick horse for ages.

He began to improve as a four-year-old and ran quite well in five races, eventually winning a claiming race at Leicester on 23 August 1995 with terrific ease at 16–1.

Henry Candy rang Peter Deal that evening and said that the good news was that Make A Stand had won . . . the bad news was that he had been claimed by Martin Pipe's assistant Chester Barnes for 8,000 guineas and the syndicate had lost him.

*   *   *

Peter Deal says, 'I had no truck with Martin Pipe for claiming Make A Stand. I have always maintained that if you run a horse in a seller or a claiming race, you risk the chance of losing the horse. That's the very reason the races are designed. The horse ran under the name of Kingstone Warren Partners, so Martin Pipe never knew at that stage that I was a part-owner. Having already had horses with Martin I felt I could ring him that night and try and get back into ownership of Make A Stand. I remember saying rather mockingly that he stood accused of nicking one of my horses, which was against the spirit of the sport. I pretended that I was terribly upset. Of course, Martin did not know the full extent of my ownership in the partnership, and said that he was terribly sorry. It was agreed that I should buy half of Make A Stand for 4,000 guineas. I was lucky as Martin really had no obligation at all to sell me a share. He had claimed the horse fair and square. I then contacted all the other owners in my syndicate and told them the situation. I offered them all a share in my half-share, but they all turned it down. The rest, as they say, is history.'

*   *   *

As a five-year-old in 1996 Make A Stand ran first for Martin Pipe on the flat at Newmarket and was a promising second. Then at

York on 15 June he won the season's richest ladies' race for Lydia Pearce as 5–2 favourite. He was always going well and took up the lead approaching the final quarter-mile, winning easily. Then Pat Eddery just got touched off by a head on him at Kempton eleven days later and he finished that flat season by coming eleventh under Michael Roberts at Newbury on 20 July. Make A Stand's hurdles debut came on 11 October 1995. He was ridden by David Bridgwater and finished ninth at 15–8 behind Kim Bailey's winner Sprung Rhythm, the 13–8 favourite. He was beaten a total of over sixty lengths that day, and *Chaseform* noted, 'Claimed off the flat by Martin Pipe, did not give any encouragement here for his hurdling career.'

'Looking back,' Peter says, 'I suppose they may have been right, but they didn't take into account the Martin Pipe factor. I suppose we would all have been accused of daydreaming if we had forecast that this was the introduction of a future Champion Hurdler.'

Make A Stand had a complete break of seven months off before he ran over hurdles again, then he set up a sequence of three wins in twenty-four days. He won his first hurdle race at Newton Abbot on 3 May by twenty-five lengths as a generous 10–1 shot. David Bridgwater rode him that day. He pulled very hard but made all to win in typical Martin Pipe style. On 15 May he won by four lengths at Huntingdon, but by now the betting public had spotted his potential and he started 5–4 favourite. That day he came from behind to win comfortably. His starting price was 11–2 on when he duly completed his quickfire hat-trick, winning by seven lengths at Hereford on 27 May, again making all for David Bridgwater, defying a double penalty.

Having ridden only one winner at the Cheltenham Festival before in two seasons, from not many rides, it had been a sensational start to the big meeting for me in 1997 when Or Royal initiated a 51–1 double on the Martin Pipe-trained dapple grey in the Guinness Arkle Challenge Trophy. While I was able to blaze a trail on Make A Stand, I knew that I had to save up Or Royal until the very last seconds to make his challenge.

I knew long before Cheltenham all about Or Royal. Martin Pipe is such a perfectionist and he leaves nothing to chance – the day he takes up roulette as a profession there will be casinos closing all over London. I had been down to Martin's lovely home to see videos of Or Royal winning over hurdles and fences in France.

I won on Or Royal in his first two races, both at Chepstow, for his new owner David Johnson, and both times I tried to keep him for a late challenge. For that first race, in November 1996, the whole world seemed to known of his potential, and he started 11–10 on favourite. I led three out, as it happened, and I had to push him all the way to the line to beat Adrian Maguire on Super Coin by a length. However, I got the feeling that although Or Royal was very classy, he was only ever going to do as much as was required. He stops when he is in front, and needs a horse to lead him virtually to the line.

In his next race at Chepstow in early December I was determined to hold him up, although it did not work out that way and I was left clear before winning by a distance. Even though you might have the greatest of race plans, they can change at one fence, or in a matter of seconds, and sometimes you end up doing exactly what you set out not to do.

If I was asked for my best riding performance of the 1996–7 season I would have to give it some thought – there were one or two I got home that were probably a shade lucky to get into the winners' enclosure. However, if pressed for my worst riding display of the season I would put my hands up and admit Or Royal in the Book of Music Novices' Chase at Ascot on 21 December 1996. I led at the twelfth fence, as I thought that Or Royal was going so well, but I got it wrong. I was soon struggling and he hung as we approached the last fence. Richard Dunwoody came and did me by three lengths on the Tim Easterby-trained Simply Dashing.

I had set the race up for Woody, which is always a grave error of judgement, as he does not turn down chances like that, but in a way it was a good thing. If I had gone for home and won I might have been tempted to kick for home in the Arkle Chase at Cheltenham, and that would surely have stuffed me.

I went to Cheltenham confident that I would ride a double. I felt that Make A Stand, who was only tipped by one of the national newspaper tipsters (plus myself), would cause a surprise, just as Martin Pipe's Granville Again had done at generous odds of 13–2 in 1993. I was sure that Or Royal would be suited by a stiffer track like Cheltenham, than by Chepstow or Ascot, and he also had the dreaded blinkers on for the first time since he joined M. C. Pipe.

If the race at Ascot had been set up for Woody, the Guinness Arkle Trophy Chase at Cheltenham was all scripted my way. If it had been a staged race it could not have gone better for Or Royal. Or Royal was much better in blinkers, although he made mistakes at the eighth fence and then again at the second last. Jamie Osborne went too soon on Squire Silk and I was able to sit in behind on Or Royal, and then pounce as we drove up the hill on the flat. I only had half a length to spare on Or Royal, but it was enough.

*   *   *

George Ennor of the *Racing Post* reported the next day: 'Or Royal, brilliantly ridden by Tony McCoy, survived two bad mistakes to win the Guinness Arkle Trophy after a thrilling tussle with Squire Silk up the famous Cheltenham hill. It was only six weeks ago that the champion jockey – whose only previous Festival win had come on Kibreet in the Grand Annual – looked in danger of missing Cheltenham after his shoulder injury at Wincanton, but the way he drove Or Royal to victory here left no doubt about his recovery.'

Trainer Andy Turnell said, 'That's twice Martin Pipe has done me,' referring to his defeat by Pipe's Cache Fleur over Turnell's Country Member in the Whitbread Gold Cup in 1995.

*   *   *

I was thrilled by Or Royal's win, especially after I had jumped off him after my first ride on him at Chepstow, and told Martin Pipe that this was an ideal horse to win the Arkle Chase. Now I feel that he has the speed and the class to be a contender for the Queen Mother Champion Two-Mile Chase at the Festival. Martin Pipe was thrilled and our little pre-race exchange seemed forgotten as he said, 'Tony McCoy has done a wonderful job. This was only Or Royal's fourth run for me.'

*   *   *

Or Royal is owned by Essex financier David Johnson, who has always been a lucky patron. Born in London's East End and an avid West Ham fan, Johnson was always keen on racing and recalls, 'I was sitting with my wife one day in the Swynford Paddocks Hotel, near Newmarket, and saw a painting of one of Robert Sangster's horses on a wall. I decided that if I was ever successful enough to own a racehorse, I would try and reverse Robert Sangster's colours, and that's exactly what I did. They didn't seem to have been too unlucky for him and they haven't done me too much harm. I was in a Coral's box at the races one day and Malcolm Palmer of the Barking-based bookmakers introduced me to the Newmarket trainer Robert Williams. I was soon talked into having a horse or two and got lucky with Pin Stripe and Café Noir.

'But my big break came in 1986 when my horse Mister Majestic won the Middle Park Stakes at Newmarket as the complete 33–1 outsider of the Group 1 field of seven. Mister Majestic had won four races earlier and had been due to run in the Mill Reef Stakes at Newbury the previous week, but he reared up in the stalls and was withdrawn, not coming under starter's orders. As Robert Williams pointed out that he had not had a race, and was very well, we let him take his chance in the Middle Park which was run that year on Newmarket's July course. I had already arranged to go to the Arc de Triomphe weekend in Paris and listened down a phone line as Ray Cochrane made all to win on Mister Majestic. I had a video of the race as shown on Channel 4, and John McCririck said, "Mister Majestic is the rag in this field and I'll eat my hat if he wins."

'Again I was in a Coral's box at the races when I mentioned to Peter Scudamore that I might like to have my first jumpers. He obviously recommended Martin Pipe, and not long after that I claimed Beebob. I must admit that at that time, in 1991–2, I had never heard of Martin Pipe, but Beebob did us well and Graham McCourt rode him to eleventh place in the 1992 Triumph Hurdle at Cheltenham. At the 1997 Festival we had the great win with Or. Royal in the Arkle Chase, but I must admit that we blew our brains out on As du Trefle in the Mildmay of Flete Chase on the Wednesday. Overnight he was a 12–1 shot and we piled so much into him that he started 100–30 favourite. However, he pulled a muscle and Tony McCoy eventually finished sixth on him as Martin Pipe's other runner Terao won the race. Going to France has been lucky for Martin and myself. We paid £82,500 for Or Royal at the Goffs Sales in Paris and I really broke the bank when I paid six figures for both Eudipe, who was second in the Sun Alliance Novices' Chase for Tony McCoy, and the highly rated Elouis. He had a bit of a setback and did not run in the 1996–7 season but he had top form in France and was rated even superior to Or Royal.

'Martin Pipe has been an outstanding trainer for me. I know that he is much maligned in some quarters, usually by people who are just jealous of his success, but I can't believe that there is a single person in racing who cares more about his horses than Martin Pipe.'

*   *   *

I thought I'd hit double top when Make A Stand and Or Royal won at Cheltenham, but Mr Mulligan was to clinch a never-to-be forgotten hat-trick just two days later.

CHAPTER 11

'Take a chance on
Mr Mulligan'

Only One Man was on everybody's lips after the 1997 Cheltenham Gold Cup day, and it was not Gordon Richards' galloping grey star. It was Tony McCoy, who took another giant step towards being the greatest jump jockey of all time when Mr Mulligan pulled off a 20–1 shock in the Festival's glittering showpiece.

One Man seemed unbeatable in the 1996 Gold Cup. He started red-hot 11–8 favourite but stopped between the last two fences as though he had been shot and trailed in sixth. In 1997 One Man drifted out to 7–1 and there were serious thoughts of running him in the Two-Mile Queen Mother Champion Chase instead. This time he did exactly the same, and having ranged up behind Mr Mulligan, his challenge died in a matter of two or three strides as Tony McCoy flew up the hill for glory on Mr Mulligan.

McCoy openly fancied Make A Stand to win the Champion Hurdle, although strangely for once Martin Pipe was not overkeen, but McCoy had doubts about Mr Mulligan after a highly disappointing gallop at Newbury. Only minutes before the Gold Cup, Mr Mulligan's genial trainer Noel Chance confided, 'I wish my horse had shown a bit more sparkle in the last few days. I don't know whether he is lazy . . . or lazy because there's something wrong with him. It's a mystery, as I had just about every vet in the south of England looking at him and we can't find anything wrong.' Within minutes of this quote, Mr Mulligan and

McCoy had galloped into the record books with a thrilling display of prominent front-running.

At only his third Festival McCoy pulled off the big race double on Make A Stand and Mr Mulligan. He became only the fourth jockey to win the two big races at the same Festival, a feat which had been achieved by Fred Winter (1961: Eborneezer and Saffron Tartan), Aubrey Brabazon (1949 and 1950: both years on Hatton's Grace and Cottage Rake), and Norman Williamson (1995: Alderbrook and Master Oats).

Mr Mulligan's win from an English-based yard saved Cheltenham from their greatest fear: Doran's Pride, Imperial Call or darling Danoli winning for Ireland. In 1996 Cheltenham's thin line of security men were as helpful as a trilby in a tornado as joyous Irishmen clambered into the winners' enclosure to greet Imperial Call and his remarkable one-legged trainer Fergie Sutherland. There were no such riots when Mr Mulligan came back. In November 1996, Edward Gillespie, Cheltenham's supremo, had revealed secret plans to install a double gate to prevent drunken gatecrashers entering the hallowed winners' circle, but strangely the proposed second gate was never introduced.

Gillespie's worst moment at the 1997 Festival came on the Wednesday, when he failed to recognise Ireland's record-breaking champion trainer Aidan O'Brien, who tried to get into the winners' enclosure to greet his Royal Sun Alliance Novices' Hurdle winner Istabraq. It was jeers and not cheers which echoed round the winners' enclosure as Irish racegoers realised that O'Brien was being barred entry. However, O'Brien, who admittedly was not carrying his official pass, did a nifty bit of hurdling himself and leapt over the railing amid loud booing from the furious Irish visitors. It was only when popular Irish trainer–TV commentator Ted Walsh dashed across to identify O'Brien that a very ugly situation was defused.

It was largely a happy 1997 Festival, although favourite-backers were left for dead in the financial gutter. With his William Hill satchels bursting at the seams with 'readies' from three very one-sided days, railsman Mike Burton grinned, 'I don't know what

*punters are worrying about. They have still got their eyes left . . .
to cry themselves all the way home!'*

However, the few backers who invested in McCoy's 167–1 big-race double were laughing all the way to the bank, and they weren't the only ones. As racegoers made their weary way home, some stuck in the annual Cheltenham car-park traffic jam for over two hours, Gillespie said, 'It's been a good meeting. To the best of my knowledge, we had no human deaths, no births – but possibly some conceptions, particularly in the Hunter's Lodge, which is the stablelads' accommodation. We might have a look at that next year.'

For thousands of racegoers and millions of Channel 4 TV viewers, however, a real star was born in Tony McCoy.

McCoy finished top jockey at the meeting with three wins, three seconds and two thirds from sixteen rides, to amass a staggering £364,037 in prize money. If you had backed all his rides you would have showed a £19.50 profit per £1 stake – largely due to Mr Mulligan, it must be said. McCoy was also the winner of the trophy given by the London Clubs Charity to the top jockey at the meeting. This was his first success as top jockey, and the trophy was presented to him by the Princess Royal.

On the night prior to his Gold Cup triumph, McCoy dined quietly at the Kilkenny Inn Brasserie at Andoversford, near Cheltenham, with Terry and Shay Chandler of Blue Thunder Apparel, Ronnie Beggan, Cameron McMillan and a few friends. McCoy was especially pleased that his girlfriend Chanelle Burke had jetted in from Ireland for Thursday's racing. She said, 'After watching Tony win the Champion Hurdle on Tuesday on Make A Stand I just couldn't stay away. I had to skip my studies for a day or two as I wanted so much to be at Cheltenham in case he won the Gold Cup.'

A day later all McCoy's dreams came true, but as he picked at his steak and sipped his usual Diet Coke, the long, lean jockey admitted, 'I'm knackered!'

McCoy was watched by a record crowd of 59,488 paying customers, an increase of twelve per cent on the 1996 crowd.

Few of them will ever forget how a twenty-two-year-old jockey
stole the Festival show on Mr Mulligan, who had not raced for
seventy-seven days, thirty of which had been on the easy list.

C.D.

Thirteen days before my Cheltenham Gold Cup win on Mr
Mulligan I was, without doubt, the unhappiest man in
racing. Noel Chance got me to ride the horse in a special gallop
at Newbury after racing – and the bottom of my world fell out.
Mr Mulligan worked so badly that on that showing he would
have been tailed off in a seller at Newton Abbot.

In mid-December I had had no firm plans for the Gold Cup. I
have always been See More Business's greatest fan, who was being
talked about as a possible Gold Cup prospect. I also knew that
M. C. Pipe was planning to enter Cyborgo in Cheltenham's
showpiece. Then Dave Roberts arranged for me to ride Mr
Mulligan in the King George VI Chase at Kempton on Boxing
Day and also at Cheltenham. My management team had nego-
tiated a deal with Guinness and Mr Mulligan's owner, Michael
Worcester, so I was committed to him.

After the Newbury gallop I was at my wits' end. Noel Chance
told everybody who bothered to stay after racing that day that Mr
Mulligan would be working with his useful hurdler Marching
Marquis. The moment I jumped on to Mr Mulligan, however, I
was sure that my galloping companion, who was ridden by Noel
Chance's assistant Alex McCabe, was not Marching Marquis,
who had just had a race at Chepstow, when he had been third
behind Boardroom Shuffle trained by Josh Gifford.

The horse I was working with, in fact, was a lowly hurdler
called Sunley Secure, who had previously been with Mick Channon on the flat and won little races at Hamilton and Goodwood.
In his last race for Noel Chance he had finished fourteenth at
Newbury the previous November, beaten by half a parish.

Noel Chance had given his girl strict orders not to head me in the two-mile gallop on the flat, but she had to hold up her horse as I struggled to get Mr Mulligan out of bottom gear. He did the worst bit of work of any horse I have ever sat on. If you had told me that thirteen days later he would win the Gold Cup, almost unchallenged by nine lengths, I would have said you were raving mad. I was scrubbing along all the way round Newbury. It was simply awful. Mr Mulligan was pushed to beat his own shadow, and it was all very embarrassing.

I must have looked like a man with a tax demand for thousands when Noel Chance greeted me afterwards. He said, 'I'm not happy.'

I replied curtly, 'You're not happy . . . what do you think I am?'

We agreed that we would tell the waiting pressmen that it was 'satisfactory', but a blind man could have seen that the whole exercise was a complete disaster. Mr Mulligan had shown no sparkle at all and I was desperately unhappy.

I went back to the jockeys' weighing-room and told Brendan Powell, 'I know what view I'm going to have of the Gold Cup – watching all the other horses' backsides as I get tailed off on Mr Mulligan.'

I was furious that I had committed myself to a horse who on that showing had no chance. If it had not been for Noel Chance and the deal with Guinness I would have moved heaven and earth to get off Mr Mulligan.

During the 1994–5 season, Mr Mulligan had just the one run when he was trained in Lambourn by Kim Bailey. He was a 10–1 shot in the Oxfordshire Novices' Chase at Newbury on 25 November 1994. Norman Williamson was something like a fence clear on him when Mr Mulligan fell at the eleventh after going well clear from the sixth. It was desperate bad luck as he looked a certain winner. He fractured a small vertebra in his neck and it was decided to give him the rest of that season off. He stayed with his owner and then joined Noel for the next season with the rest of Michael Worcester's horses.

*   *   *

Noel recalls, 'Michael Worcester was always very keen on Mr Mulligan and told me boldly that he could turn out to be one of the best chasers in England. As a new trainer for an important owner I, of course, nodded and agreed, eager to impress my new boss. Mr Mulligan was showing plenty of speed at home and I decided that the best way to please my new guv'nor was to try and win first time out with him.

'After Mr Mulligan's crashing fall at Newbury the previous season, the number one target was to get his confidence back. He was impressing me at home and I decided to run him first time for me over hurdles. We selected the Green 'Un Novices' Hurdle at Uttoxeter on 20 September 1995, where he started at 11–2 and I was quite prepared to have a few quid on him.

'Mr Mulligan made every yard of the running that day and I began to get a little excited. He won again over hurdles at Wetherby and then he made a winning chasing debut by a distance in the hands of Mark Dwyer. By then his full potential was beginning to get known and he started 6–5 that day.'

*   *   *

Mr Mulligan was due to run in the valuable Feltham Novices' Chase at Kempton on Boxing Day that year, but the meeting was a victim of the weather. He then won the Towton Novices' Chase at Wetherby on 11 January 1996 by fifteen lengths, and thoughts turned to the big Cheltenham Festival. Next stop for him was the Reynoldstown Chase at Ascot on 14 February. Noel claims he never had him as good as he was that day not even when I won the Cheltenham Gold Cup on him. Richard Johnson again made all on him and he beat Jenny Pitman's Nahthen Lad by fifteen lengths, with horses such as Major Summit, future Grand National winner Lord Gyllene, and Go Ballistic trailing in way behind him.

He was then made 11–8 favourite for the Sun Alliance Novices' Chase at Cheltenham and was everybody's idea of the banker bet at the 1996 Festival. Sadly, it all went wrong for Richard Johnson when he was knocked going into the first, made a series of mistakes through running too freely, and was finally eight lengths second to Nahthen Lad.

Noel Chance is a splendid Dublin-born man who came to Folly House stables, Lambourn, after a real globe-trotting career. He arrived at the yard owned by the family of thriller writer Dick Francis on May Day 1995, and quickly became a familiar figure at the English tracks.

He is quite a character. In December 1996 I was riding and missed the the annual Horserace Writers' Association lunch in London, when I won the jump jockeys' award. Noel made his debut appearance, and holds the unusual record of attending the lunch . . . and ending up in another country on the same day! Noel was seated at a very dangerous table with a group of lively Lambourn personalities, who were all keen to make it a day to remember.

They lunched well and Noel later fell asleep on the train back to Swindon, only to wake up in the railway sidings at Newport in Wales. He found his way back to the station where he bumped into two winos in the waiting-room and was scared out of his life, as he was still carrying 'a nice few quid'. Happily he did not get mugged and caught the 4.29 morning train back to Swindon. He hailed the first taxi on the rank at the station, and walked into his stables just as his first lot were pulling out. He's a real Irish stayer!

Noel was apprenticed to Sir Hugh Nugent in Ireland and later started training after emigrating to Australia at twenty-five years old with 'just six quid in his pocket'. He worked in Sydney for an extraordinary trainer called Vic Thompson. Noel recalls, 'Vic had suffered a head injury and was completely mad. He used to rant and rave. He spied on us when we started work in the darkness at four o'clock in the morning. I lasted two weeks.'

Noel returned to Ireland and started training with just three horses on the former Dublin racecourse at Phoenix Park. The Pope put a stop to all that, however: for his visit to the Park thousands of stakes were banged into the ground to control the vast crowd – right in the middle of Noel's hallowed gallops. Half a million people turned up and churned up the gallops. He jokes, 'The Pope went home, but the holes in the ground stayed . . . and that was my lot. I moved to the Curragh and then on to Lambourn. You can say that it was the Pope who got me going to England and the win with Mr Mulligan and Tony McCoy.'

Actually, it was Bristol-based owner Michael Worcester who lured Noel Chance to England with the offer of being his private trainer at Lambourn. He jumped at the opportunity and says, 'I'm a great survivor. I believe that when one door closes, another one always opens.' He has done well for Michael Worcester who has made his fortune from the ice-cream-cone business.

Nearer the time of the Cheltenham Festival I went down to Noel Chance's stables at Lambourn. Mr Mulligan worked over nine fences and seemed to be a different horse. I even joked to his trainer, 'What have you got here, a ringer?' although there was no disguising Mr Mulligan's prominent white colourings.

With his flaxen mane he looked like Roy Rogers' Trigger. Purists will say that Mr Mulligan has too much white about him. When his owner was persuaded to buy him on the phone from Ireland, he was told, 'Send a cheque now for £18,000. If you see all his white colourings, you'll never buy him.'

I was slightly heartened by this piece of work but still not over the moon at the prospect of riding him in the Gold Cup, and all the time the word was that Cyborgo's owners were keen to run in the Gold Cup, especially if there was rain.

*   *   *

It was a worrying period for Noel Chance, who confesses, 'Nearer the time that Mr Mulligan worked so badly I was nearly suicidal. All the vibes from his work at Lambourn were negative. Martin Pipe still had Cyborgo and Challenger Du Luc in the Gold Cup entries and I was constantly asked if Tony McCoy was still going to ride for me. I kept my mouth shut and never said a word, but I made one phone call to Dave Roberts, who said that our arrangement was still on, and that was good enough for me. I never had much doubt that Tony would ride Mr Mulligan in the

Gold Cup, although I could see that he might by tempted by Cyborgo, especially on heavy ground. I was slightly worried when I realised that Tony had fallen out with Paul Nicholls and Paul Barber over his keenness to ride Martin Pipe's horse rather than one of theirs, but Tony's management team had done a deal with Guinness and so he came down to Lambourn to ride work and be photographed with Mr Mulligan.

'But for Tony's column in the *Sun*, nobody would have known that he was due to ride Mr Mulligan on Saturday, 1 March after racing at Newbury just thirteen days before the Cheltenham Festival. It was a nightmare experience and I was never so low as when I drove home after that gallop. Even though I told the press guys a few white lies, there was no concealing our disappointment. Mr Mulligan had worked like an absolute donkey and I quite expected the dreaded phone call from Tony begging to get off the horse for one of Martin Pipe's. Every time the phone rang I feared the worst, but thankfully the young man never called.

'After the terrible Newbury gallop, I persuaded Tony to come down to Lambourn and pop Mr Mulligan over a few fences. Once the horse saw a few fences he put up a much better display. Then on the Sunday prior to Cheltenham I decided to work Mr Mulligan on what is called the Home Gallop at Lambourn, which is on the side of a hill. My stablelad Timmy Murphy rode Mr Mulligan – again against an inferior horse – and he worked like a dream. The moment the old bugger realised that he was heading for home he suddenly clicked up a gear and it ended with him nearly pulling Timmy Murphy's arms out.'

*   *   *

I had to cling to the memory of Mr Mulligan's display in the King George VI Chase at Kempton on Boxing Day, my only previous ride on him. I knew from Noel Chance that his preparation for that race had been another disaster: for three weeks he had suffered what amounted to a hole in his foot. Noel said of him, 'He was so brave that he never went lame and showed us what was wrong in his pre-race gallops. Given the injury before the Christmas race I was amazed by how long he kept up his tremendous gallop round Kempton. He had been a dodgy jumper before, but that day he left his earlier poor run at Chepstow behind him and really seemed to enjoy himself at the front of affairs. At one stage I glanced round and saw that I really had the entire field strung out.

Three fences out Richard Dunwoody sailed up to me on One Man and I knew that my chances of actually winning on Mr Mulligan, who was at that stage an ex-crock, were pretty slight, but Mr Mulligan kept galloping on and I was assured of second place until falling at the last. Maybe I was a bit too keen, but I always had it in my mind that perhaps One Man might stop. I was only six lengths adrift at the last when we fell.

Richard Dunwoody went on to win a record fourth King George VI – all on greys, including Desert Orchid – and One Man lowered the course record set by Cuddy Dale in 1991 by half a second. Maybe I was responsible for that record, as Mr Mulligan had done all the donkey work up at the front, but I was not too disappointed. I felt in my heart that if Mr Mulligan had not blown-up – and had jumped the last – we might even have beaten One Man.

I was furious at costing Mr Mulligan's connections the assured £25,000 for second place, but I was not as sick as poor Adrian Maguire when he fell on Barton Bank in the same race back in 1994 with victory absolutely assured.

*   *   *

Noel Chance says of that race, 'I only had him seventy-five per cent right for the King George VI and he had virtually no preparation, but Tony gave him a superb ride round Kempton. Mr Mulligan loved going along at the head of affairs and at one stage he really had the field strung out. One Man finally collared Mr Mulligan at the third last and we were about six lengths down at the last when Mr Mulligan fell. I rushed down to meet Tony and he put his hands up straightaway and said that it was his fault.

He was very sorry and admitted that we would have easily got the £25,000 for second place if he had just popped him over the last fence and been a bit more cautious. But Tony knew, like me, that there was always the chance that One Man might not get home. Tony threw everything into the last fence and for once it did not come off. Tony kept saying to me, "I'll ride him in the Gold Cup and I swear that One Man will never beat us again."

'I was thrilled with Mr Mulligan's display, even though we went home without a shilling in prize money. With my old pal Terry Casey deciding to let Rough Quest run, I had thought that we might sneak fourth place. I knew how desperate Mr Mulligan's preparation had been. I must admit that when I got home I did have a serious rush of blood. I rang the bookies Sean Graham in Belfast and had a few quid on Mr Mulligan at 20–1 for the Gold Cup. After what Tony McCoy had said, I thought he was an absolute certainty.'

*   *   *

I have to admit that while I thought Mr Mulligan would run well in the Gold Cup, my own fancy to win the race was Imperial Call, who had won the Cheltenham showpiece the year before.

The *Sun* headlines on Gold Cup day read, 'Mr Mulli can make frame' and in my column I said, 'Take A Chance On Me to get to No. 1', a reference to Mr Mulligan's trainer and the hit single of pop group Abba. After Tuesday's wins on Make A Stand and Or Royal, I was still on cloud nine, and I added:

> I'd love to emulate Norman Williamson and win both the Champion Hurdle and Gold Cup, like he did on Alderbrook and Master Oats. I give Mr Mulligan a real chance, and at 16–1 he is knocking each-way value. Imperial Call is undoubtedly the main danger. The ground changed to 'good to firm' yesterday and that will certainly help Imperial Call. Mr Mulligan usually forces the pace, but with Dublin Flyer in the race I may be able to tuck my horse in behind the confirmed front-runner.
>
> Mr Mulligan's biggest advantage is that he has not run since Kempton on Boxing Day. He will be the freshest horse in the race.

Noel Chance believes that he has him spot on to run the race of his life. I galloped him at Newbury recently, and to be honest he didn't set the world alight, but Richard Johnson, who has ridden him before, encourages me by saying that he's worked like a slacker before and then come out and roared home in big races like the Reynoldstown Chase at Ascot last season.

I'm hoping that Mr Mulligan can repeat Dawn Run's effort in 1986, who unseated Tony Mullins in her race prior to the Gold Cup, and then came out and won the Festival's greatest event. Take A Chance On Me . . . let's hope Mr Mulligan is on song to go to No. 1.

I had the shock of my life before the Gold Cup. I walked out to the paddock to meet owner Michael Worcester and Noel Chance and had a close look at Mr Mulligan as he was being walked round. I didn't think that he looked that special; there were hairy bits on his coat. Of course, having lots of white he always catches the eye. As I was given the leg-up by Noel Chance, we heard that Mr Mulligan had won the prize for the best turned-out horse in the Gold Cup. I couldn't believe it. I don't know who did the judging but I hope he didn't trip over his white stick on his way out!

Happily, the moment Mr Mulligan made his way out on to the course for the parade in front of the packed grandstands, he really came to life. All the old spark seemed to have returned.

Down at the start I looked across and saw my great buddy Charlie Swan, who was on Martin Pipe's Cyborgo. I told Charlie, 'This fella of mine feels great. If he gets round, I won't be beaten.' It was an odd conversation, as two weeks before I would have given my right arm to have ridden Cyborgo instead of Mr Mulligan. Now the supreme irony was to unfold.

The plan was to let Dublin Flyer charge off in front and to allow Mr Mulligan to go at his own pace. My first concern was not to let Cheltenham frighten Mr Mulligan in any way. The previous year his chances had been blundered away and his confidence was knocked at the very first fence.

Mr Mulligan jumped far better than in his previous races. Although he clouted the fourth last, by then he had most of his rivals in trouble. Dublin Flyer was only in contention on the first circuit and was eventually pulled up before the second last fence. Mr Mulligan is a big, long horse and he can be a bit clumsy, but if you make sure that his stride is accurate, he can really ping them. He's got the ability to be a really great horse. We had taken the lead at the thirteenth, the water, and I realised turning up the final hill that victory was in his grasp. He galloped all the way to the line to beat Barton Bank by nine lengths, with Doran's Pride back in third. One Man loomed at one stage, but he finished a disappointing sixth, and connections must now accept that he simply does not stay. Imperial Call was never going well and was pulled up when tailed off six fences from home, and Danoli fell two out. Cyborgo was last of the eighteen finishers, with six horses failing to complete. Mr Mulligan won at 20–1.

After the win I went to the Royal Box to meet The Queen Mother, accompanied by Chanelle, Noel Chance and the horse's winning connections. They were magic moments, but with the great excitement it's all a bit of a blur looking back. I know that I ordered two cases of champagne for the weighing-room . . . and sipped Diet Coke while the other jocks all went raving mad.

There must have been some happy *Sun* punters that day with the 20–1 starting price. The biggest recorded bet on the course was £18,000 to £1,000.

One man who was cheering Mr Mulligan on was Upper Lambourn trainer Brian Meehan. Before the Gold Cup he had a £25 double on Mr Mulligan with his Lincoln Handicap hope Tumbleweed Ridge. Meehan explains, 'I'm not that partial to gambling and only have a few quid on mine when I really fancy them, but I know Noel Chance, and all the word in Lambourn was that Mr Mulligan was fancied. I had a contact with Noel, as I had been the trainer at Folly House stables, Lambourn, before he took over. For a £25 outlay, the thought of Noel and myself winning the Gold Cup and the Lincoln was too much of a temptation. I would have won £11,000 as I backed them both when they were 20–1. It seemed like a nice spring bet.' Mr Mulligan duly landed the first leg, but Tumbleweed Ridge, having been backed from an ante-post 25–1, ran a blinder in the Lincoln as 7–1 joint favourite to finish third behind short-head winner Kuala Lips.

After my win on Mr Mulligan I heard a lot of stories of punters who had backed him at big prices. I was chuffed to think that I had made so many people happy. Perhaps the happiest punter on the track was Sussex-based Clive Hacking, brother of Folkestone and Lingfield steward Robert Hacking. Clive, a former rugby international trialist with Blackheath in his younger days, was at Cheltenham to support his nephew Paul, who rode the pulled-up Colonial Kelly in the Foxhunters, which he has won earlier in his career on Certain Light. Clive decided to splash out a pound from his Romney Marsh fortune to invest on just one ticket on the placepot at Cheltenham. He selected six horses, including Gold Cup winner Mr Mulligan, and just needed Major Bell to be in the first three in the sixth event, the Cathcart. Major Bell was second – I was third on Or Royal – and Hacking sent his daughter down to collect the Tote's placepot winnings, telling her, 'It will be about a grand.'

Imagine the glee of the family when a gushing Tote official said, 'I'm afraid we will have to pay you half cash, and half cheque.'

Miss Hacking asked, 'How much is it?'

The reply came . . . £6,227.50.

My day wasn't over with the Gold Cup, however, and apart from the third on Or Royal in the Cathcart, I had a second on Elzoba in the Grand Annual. I won the London Clubs Charity award for the top jockey at the Festival with three wins. Richard Dunwoody also had three wins, but I had had three second placings and Woody did not finish runner-up at all during the meeting.

Many Irish punters went wild with delight after the Gold Cup, as they had backed Mr Mulligan at 20–1 because Noel Chance and myself both hail from the Emerald Isle. In the *Daily Express* John Garnsey reported:

One day the Champion Hurdle, two days later the Cheltenham Tote Gold Cup. Yet amid the cheers and euphoria of the greatest double in National Hunt racing, Tony McCoy, the man who made it all happen, was the most relaxed Irishman at the Festival. He was back in the winners' enclosure after his superb Gold Cup triumph on Mr Mulligan – achieved in almost identical style to his Champion Hurdle victory two days earlier on Make A Stand. But, in contrast to the wild-eyed exuberance of so many of his fellow countrymen, McCoy sat quietly through his press conference, speaking in a voice barely above a whisper and not bothering to sip his celebration champagne. He had, by all accounts, been in the same mood the night before at a party to celebrate Make A Stand's victory, when he told a friend, 'All I want to do is go to bed.' This was not the reaction of a twenty-two-year-old tired of life, or indeed one indifferent to the great rewards being champion jockey has brought him. It was simply a true professional focusing himself for the task ahead. His dedication will make him one of the all-time greats.

Cheltenham had indeed been good to me, and by winning three races worth £364,036 you don't have to be a genius to work out what my win money in three days came to at ten per cent.

*　　*　　*

Noel Chance recalls that day: 'It took me twenty years in Ireland to train a hundred winners, and it was always an unequal struggle with five or six trainers having eighty per cent of the horses, but Mr Mulligan made it all worthwhile. I watched the race by myself in the owners' and trainers' stand. I never stand with my actual owners or my wife – it's a superstition. I'm not a great man for publicity and did not realise that the TV cameras were on me.

'I had told Tony to pop Mr Mulligan off and not to force him – if Dublin Flyer wanted to make the pace, that was fine. I could see that Tony jumped the first two fences on a perfect stride, and I was pretty sure from that point that Mr Mulligan would win. I did not realise it, but I was standing next to Unguided Missile's owners. When they fell at the thirteenth fence, they were sporting enough to tell me that they then hoped that I would win.

'I've watched the race hundreds of times since, as our village postman in Lambourn is a video buff, and edited all the Gold Cup coverage of the day down to thirty-five minutes. The amazing thing is that Tony McCoy had Mr Mulligan so perfectly balanced at every single fence. He had the horse taking the fences on a stride at every obstacle. I never feared One Man for a moment. The only horse I saw as a danger as they turned for home was Doran's Pride, who eventually finished third behind the runner-up Barton Bank.

'Tony is such a natural horseman – he's something else. He has a great hunger for the game and to ride winners, but you never see him abusing a horse to fulfil his burning ambition.

'After some of my experiences of parties, I was determined not to go too mad after the Gold Cup. I made sure all my staff were invited to a special celebration that night at my local – the Queen's at East Garston. It was quite a party. Tony was invited but did not come. I guess he was sipping his Diet Coke whilst providing champagne for all the other jockeys in a Cheltenham nightclub! I always joked that I was bankrolling the Guinness sponsorship myself after all the gallons of the black stuff I have downed over the years.

'To this day the Gold Cup win has not really sunk in. It has not done my business any harm and I start the 1997–8 season with all my twenty-six boxes full. I owe a great debt to Mr Mulligan.

'A jinx seems to have hit Gold Cup winners, but perhaps Mr Mulligan has had his jinx season in the one when he won his first Gold Cup. Although there was not much more that could have gone wrong, he still managed to win the big race, which will obviously be his target again in 1998. We will not shrink from any challenges along the way, and I'd love him to win the King George VI Chase at Kempton on Boxing Day. I'm not blaming Tony for one minute, but that £25,000 is the prize money that escaped from under our noses.'

*   *   *

As always seems to happen these days, the 'knockers' were soon out after Mr Mulligan's win. Critics claimed that he had beaten a field of novices (Doran's Pride, Cyborgo and Danoli!), One Man clearly did not stay and all was not well with Dublin Flyer and Imperial Call, who were both pulled up. But Mr Mulligan, although drifting from 12–1 out to 25–1 and back to a 20–1 starting price, was the each-way choice of many happy punters. A horse can do no more than win a Gold Cup by nine lengths, although the snipers will point out that 33–1 runner-up Barton Bank was going in his seventeenth race since his last win.

After the Gold Cup Mr Mulligan was rated seven pounds inferior to Imperial Call, who had won the race the previous year. This time Christopher Mordaunt, the official British Horse-racing Board handicapper, raised Mr Mulligan ten pounds to 168, while Imperial Call was given 175 after his win.

Noel Chance took the new rating with a typical cheerful smile and observed, 'I've become accustomed to moaning when the handicapper puts my horses too high, so I'm not going to get too hot under the collar this time. They can crab Mr Mulligan's win, but they have all forgotten the endless problems he had with his back and then his sore feet. So many things went wrong that I can't remember half of them myself. Ten days before Cheltenham he even had a dirty nose.

'I am certain that Mr Mulligan is a ten-pound better horse than the one Tony McCoy rode to win the Gold Cup. I know for sure that Mr Mulligan was not at the same high level of form when he won last season's Reynoldstown Chase at Ascot. I just hope that all the same horses whom Mr Mulligan beat in the Gold Cup turn up at Kempton for the 1997 King George VI Chase on Boxing Day. Then we'll really show them what Mr Mulligan can do.'

Christopher Mordaunt claimed, 'Mr Mulligan's Gold Cup win was not as good as some winners over the past ten years, but he is certainly up to the Gold Cup average and perhaps on a par with Garrison Savannah. I would not label him a bad winner. There are very few Gold Cup winners who record an exceptional rating the first time they win it. I hope that Mr Mulligan is the type to go on and win a second Gold Cup.'

Mr Mulligan now has to prove the history books wrong. Irish-trained L'Escargot, way back in 1970 and 1971, is the last chaser to win back-to-back Gold Cups. There seems to be an uncanny jinx on Gold Cup winners defending their crown. The Dikler, Forgive 'N Forget and Charter Party all went back as champions, only to be placed. The Fellow finished second twice, before finally winning in 1994, but also failed when defending his title. The hoodoo goes deeper, as Imperial Call and Master Oats – the last two Gold Cup winners prior to Mr Mulligan – failed to win a race afterwards up to the end of the 1996–7 campaign. Winning the Blue Riband of steeplechasing clearly takes a heavy toll, but hopefully Mr Mulligan will end the jinx.

Being a jump jockey is like a game of snakes and ladders. You either experience the thrills of the ups, or the cruel depression of the downs. At times there does not seem to be a middle between the two extremes.

After the highs of Cheltenham I was due at Folkestone on the Friday. I guess I felt a lot better than some of the other jockeys who had been celebrating Mr Mulligan's Gold Cup win, but I was drained and tired. The thought of a few moderate rides at Folkestone was not helped by the usual multi-car pile-up and traffic jam on the M25. After I finished eighth out of nine finishers in the opening claiming hurdle on Jim Neville's Minster's Madam, I really came back to earth with a bang when Newlands-General dumped me three fences from home in the handicap chase. I managed to get over this fall and was third on Ken Higson's Swinging Sixties, and down the field on Golden Lily in the bumper race. After the excitement of Cheltenham, the joys of little Folkestone did seem a shade tame.

However, the *Sun* hired a glittering crown for a day after Mr Mulligan's win and I was pictured wearing it on the scales at Folkestone. Jamie Osborne was kept waiting to get weighed out for the first race and laughed, 'You'll want a grand for that exclusive picture . . . only because you'll look such a prat!'

The following Tuesday at Uttoxeter my world really did fall apart when I was signed off by the course doctor Andy Toman after being knocked unconscious. I went through the wing of the first hurdle on Martin Pipe-trained Strong Tel in the SQ Magazine National Hunt Novices' Hurdle. I lay prostrate for some time, and when the runners came around on the second circuit they had to be waved round me. Eventually I got to my feet and was helped back to the ambulance room. Because I had been knocked unconscious for up to three minutes, it was officially decided that I should be stood down for ten days – but that's another story.

*   *   *

Tony McCoy received plenty of glowing praise for his Cheltenham big race double. In his column in the *Daily Telegraph* at the end of the memorable Festival, John Oaksey wrote:

> Humans were involved at Cheltenham, too, of course, and I am not the only observer who reckons that the standard of jockeymanship was at least as high as any within living memory. There may have been individuals better than Messrs Dunwoody, Osborne, McCoy, Swan or Williamson – and, of course, the poor luckless Adrian Maguire who was absent yet again – but as the cast for jumping's greatest drama, I doubt if this lot has ever, collectively, been excelled. To write that a top-class jump jockey 'ought to take better care of himself' sounds not only a contradiction in terms, but also a bit like suggesting that he should take up some less hazardous profession.
>
> No one in his senses would dream, at this moment, of suggesting this to Tony McCoy, but I still think his present ten-day suspension on account of concussion might be a blessing in disguise.
>
> The fact is that Toby Balding was not far wrong the other day when he said of his precociously talented protégé from County Antrim: 'Tony is sometimes too brave for his own good.' Cheltenham also made it clearer than ever, to quote Balding again, that McCoy 'has a ready made racing brain'. It was gloriously apparent as he played the Champion Hurdle field like a master angler with a fish on a tight line. Nor would anyone intent on 'taking better care of himself' have accepted the ride on Mr Mulligan in the first place.

I had the privilege of watching the Gold Cup beside John Francome, seven times champion and the best negotiator of a steeplechase fence I have ever seen. 'Incredible,' he said, referring to McCoy's handling of the winner, Mr Mulligan. 'And don't forget that Mr Mulligan is not everybody's idea of an easy ride. Tony organised him from the first fence to the last. Kick or sit still, he got it right nearly every time, and made two mistakes look nothing.'

After watching the big races as the guest of Ladbroke's in their private box, former Irish flat champion jockey Christy Roche told guests, 'Tony McCoy should be handicapped, he's that much better than all his rivals. It's unfair that other jockeys have to take on McCoy at level weights. It's not horses who should be "handicapped" but McCoy.'

John Francome wrote in the *Sun*:

McCoy is quite outstanding. McCoy is the best jockey I have ever seen, since the days of my career in the saddle or since I retired.

He is unbelievable and I have never seen a better Gold Cup ride than the one he gave Mr Mulligan. He made a very difficult ride look easy. McCoy is so positive – that's his secret. He had Mr Mulligan spot on at every fence and gained untold lengths on the way round. When I heard Christy Roche make his remark that it's not horses but McCoy who should be handicapped, both I and Irish trainer John Mulhern nodded in agreement. I never believed that I was the world's greatest jockey, although I admit that I might have been the shrewdest.

John McCririck said, 'In my view, at this stage of his career McCoy is almost the world's greatest jockey, but perhaps in a few years' time I will have to demote John Francome.

'Punters have so much respect for Tony McCoy. He is the pin-up boy of the betting shops – backers include him in doubles and trebles without even looking at the form of his horses. They back McCoy blind. There are not many jockeys who gain this accolade, perhaps only Lester Piggott and now Frankie Dettori. What is amazing about McCoy is that he is so cool for a twenty-two-year-old. He presents an excellent image for racing and, as an ambassador, he is a great credit to the sport.'

*　　*　　*

Martin Pipe's four winners at the 1997 Cheltenham Festival equalled the record previously held by Tom Coulthwaite way back in 1923. As well as my wins on Or Royal and Make A Stand, Martin Pipe also scored with Big Strand and Terao. The leading Festival trainer is the late Fulke Walwyn, who had forty winners between 1946 and 1986, but Martin went past current trainers David Nicholson, Edward O'Grady and Nicky Henderson. Later Henderson won with Barna Boy to equal Martin's record of eighteen Festival wins. Interestingly, both Coulthwaite and Pipe had non-racing backgrounds. Coulthwaite was an athletics coach prior to switching to racing, and Pipe is the bookie's son who has become the most prolific record-breaking trainer jump racing has ever known. Coulthwaite never sat on a horse in his life but still trained three Grand National winners.

*　　*　　*

In the edition of the *Weekender* after Cheltenham, Julian Muscat wrote:

Much has been written about Tony McCoy's riding skills, and deservedly so. He has the fire of youth in his belly, and he emphasised that to be in the saddle is most definitely a game for the young. I believe the alliance between McCoy and Martin Pipe, destined to run for some time, will ensure that Pipe lands the very few jump races of note missing from his record so far.

McCoy is the first Pond House stables rider since Peter Scudamore to exploit Pipe's unmatched skill at extracting the last ounce from his horses. McCoy's ability to dictate races from the front is particularly well suited to Pipe's horses. He rides them accordingly, as he did on Make A Stand in the Champion Hurdle. Despite his forceful style of running, Make A Stand has the priceless ability to find another gear in the closing stages. With hindsight, it is significant that McCoy was not on board Make A Stand – getting thirteen pounds – when finishing only fifth behind Space Trucker at Cheltenham in November.

After the win on Mr Mulligan the press were in high spirits. In the *Sporting Life* the next day Alistair Down wrote: 'At home on the gallops your granny would leave Mr Mulligan struggling in the slipstream of her Zimmer. But under a do-or-die ride from Tony McCoy, Mr Mulligan proved far too good for the best chasers these islands have to offer in the Cheltenham Gold Cup. It was McCoy's meeting. Chance's day.'

In the *Racing Post* Brough Scott reported:

Talent is not enough. Other jockeys may have had the balance and timing and horsemanship of A. P. McCoy, certainly some have been neater. But rarely if ever have we had anyone with compulsion to match. This is a driven man. Mr Mulligan, like Make A Stand, knew what it's like to be a driven horse. The key to McCoy is that while he may be obsessive, he is anything but moronic. This is no head-down, eyes-shut horse flogger. This is a winner prepared to search every angle, as well as stretch every sinew for victory, and the joy for the history-watchers at Cheltenham was that twice in three days he found a horse to match his commitment. Many jockeys under ultimate pressure get loose and flappy; McCoy only clamps in tighter still. It takes terrific strength to apply such short-leathered leg-thrusting. Watch the video, see the message of mind and muscle. It is a signal that we now have a champion to match any that have gone before.

*   *   *

Ronnie Beggan and Cameron McMillan organised a superb party for me at the end of the 1996–7 campaign on 14 June at Newbury racecourse. The season was just over and I was thrilled at the turn-out of four hundred guests to celebrate winning the Tote Cheltenham Gold Cup, Champion Hurdle and a second full championship title. The occasion was supported by the *Sporting Life*, *Hello!* magazine, Guinness and

Blue Thunder Apparel. I received a standing ovation when I turned up after riding Blair Castle to win at Market Rasen in the new season, and was astonished to see how many jockeys and friends were in the room. I felt very honoured that so many colleagues had made the effort to join in the celebration. I was particularly pleased to see my Irish chums Adrian Maguire and Norman Williamson there. We were also lucky to have the Derby-winning jockey Willie Ryan, who had just won the Epsom Classic on Benny The Dip, amongst the partygoers. Also present was Henry Cecil's new stable jockey and fellow Irishman Kieren Fallon.

Without doubt the evening was made for me when my parents suddenly appeared. I had no idea they were there, and it was like *This Is Your Life*. My mother is simply terrified of flying and had never set foot in England before, so it was a great occasion. I thought it was a miracle when I saw my mother walking across the room, and I'll never forget the proud look on her face. I guess as Mick Channon once said, 'The boy done good.'

I was so pleased to see Noel Chance and Michael Worcester, the trainer and owner of Mr Mulligan, joining in the fun. They received a barrel of Guinness. Martin Pipe was also there, and Peter Deal, the owner of Make A Stand, whom he always refers to simply as 'Stanley'.

The free Guinness seemed to flow well and my fellow guests produced some real hellraising on the dancefloor as the revelry lasted into the early hours.

It wasn't quite my scene, however. There was booze flowing everywhere, but as usual I didn't have a drop. The long, hard season had taken its toll and I preferred to sit with my family and Chanelle and watch all the others enjoying themselves. Perhaps that old greed was not far away, as I started thinking of my third jockeys' title, passing two hundred winners for the season, and winning my first Grand National.

CHAPTER 12

'I knew there was no IRA bomb at the Grand National'

A supreme irony surrounded the IRA's bomb hoax which caused the 1997 Grand National to be abandoned on Saturday, 5 April, and run on the following Monday instead. It came during a rare low point in Tony McCoy's ever-upward career, as the Jockey Club ban meant that he had to miss the big Aintree three-day meeting. McCoy was employed by BBC TV at Aintree, but there was no doubt that he was itching to get back into the real action. However, a twist of fate resulted in Paul Nicholls' Belmont King missing the rescheduled Grand National, enabling him to take his chance a fortnight later in the Scottish National, when Tony was back from his enforced rest. Denied a run at Aintree, north of the border Tony made up for the disappointment and won the Ayr race on Belmont King.

Having won the two big races at the Cheltenham Festival, it is understandable that McCoy now says, 'To win the Grand National is my greatest ambition. I have yet to get round in my two tries, but I am sure that Belmont King will be an ideal candidate. He showed at Ayr that he can handle firmish ground and is not the out-and-out soft-ground specialist we all imagined.'

The final day of the 1996–7 season, 31 May, saw McCoy officially crowned as champion at Stratford-on-Avon. A blazing sun shone brightly down on the Midlands track, but the heat was off for the Irishman. He had been well clear of all rivals for virtually every day of the season. Before the last day's racing, wearing the familiar Blue Thunder baseball cap, he received the keys of a shiny new £28,000 Saab from the company's Great Britain managing director Will Edwyn-Jones. He also received a beautiful set of George III silver spurs mounted on a mahogany base.

McCoy, never one really to enjoy a posse of photographers, was snapped for endless minutes inside and outside his new car. His drawn face began to look very bored until a wag shouted, 'Imagine that Richard Dunwoody has retired!' The friendly smile quickly returned.

There was very much an end-of-term atmosphere about Stratford's annual final meeting, although on a blisteringly hot day the course produced a major coup by having no ice available for thirsty racegoers. Before racing, the track's new grandstand was opened by John Oaksey. His Lordship spoke in glowing terms about the new stand, although as a short man, John would not have enjoyed being in the grandstand to watch a race – he wouldn't have seen a thing. The steps are so shallow that all racegoers can see is the back of the person's head in front of them.

For McCoy, obviously tired after a long season, there was no grandstand finish. When he was injured, there had been speculation that Jamie Osborne might mount a serious threat for the title. Osborne did enjoy a purple patch, but he was never going to catch McCoy.

On that last day of the season at Stratford, McCoy made all in typical style on Martin Pipe's Doualago. Pipe was in very relaxed mood, and the next day his wife Carol grinned, 'We've had our summer holiday. I persuaded Martin actually to stay away from home for one night after the evening meeting at Stratford last night!'

McCoy finished the season with 190 winners, well clear of his nearest rival Jamie Osborne (131). It was a strike rate of twenty-nine per cent winners. Seventy-seven of his winners came for

Martin Pipe from 219 rides – a strike rate of thirty-five per cent. McCoy had won £1,289,011 in prize money and yet another record had been established.

C.D.

I'll never forget the evening of Monday, 24 March 1997 when my beloved Arsenal were robbed of their last real chance of winning the Premier Division title. Because of a giant-sized Jockey Club medical cock-up, that same evening I was robbed of the chance of riding in the Martell Grand National at Aintree.

I had gone through the wing of the first hurdle in the SQ Magazine National Hunt Novices' Hurdle at Uttoxeter on 18 March, when Martin Pipe's Strong Tel, who had been well backed at 3–1, ducked out at the last second. The fall resulted in my being knocked unconscious. Racecourse doctor Andy Toman signed me off for ten days, which meant that my next big target – the Grand National on 5 April – was safe. Even though I had been unconscious for a period of time, I eventually walked to the ambulance, then back into the weighing-room, and was allowed to drive home without the merest suggestion of an X-ray or a visit to hospital, or that I shouldn't be behind the wheel of a car for the near three-hour drive home on busy motorways.

It was learned later that Dr Toman had made an error of judgement in giving me ten days. According to the amount of time I was unconscious I should either have been suspended for seven days – or twenty-one! Some difference, and how the doctor ever arrived at ten days is a secret between him and his stethoscope. Obviously, I was not able to say for sure how long I was knocked out, but I was not falling about like a drunk afterwards and managed to drive home. I did not believe that there was anything too seriously wrong with me, and indeed I was at Toby Balding's stables the very next morning to ride two lots of work. I felt fine.

However, watching Arsenal play Liverpool on TV as I lay on the couch at home in Weyhill, where I lived then, I feared the worst. The race for the Premier Division title became a two-horse one between Liverpool and Manchester United after referee Gerald Ashby gave Liverpool the cushiest penalty-kick award of all time. It was such a bad decision, that even Liverpool's Robbie Fowler, who had clashed with Arsenal goalie David Seaman, begged the referee not to award the spot-kick.

Seaman blocked Fowler's penalty kick, but Liverpool's Jason McAteer slammed in the rebound and the Merseysiders went on to win 2–1. The controversial penalty put paid to Arsenal's championship chances and I felt sick for them. My support for them goes back to my childhood in Northern Ireland, when so many of their players seemed to be Irish, including my special hero at the time, goalkeeper Pat Jennings.

If I felt despair at Arsenal getting beaten after playing so well, my world fell apart shortly after ten o'clock that evening when I received the one telephone call I was dreading. Dr Michael Turner, the Jockey Club's chief medical officer, rang to inform me officially that because it had been adjudged that I had been unconscious for one minute after my fall at Uttoxeter the previous Tuesday, I would automatically be stood down for twenty-one days. This meant – and Dr Turner was decent enough to voice his regrets – that I was barred from riding in the Grand National.

To say I was disappointed would be putting it mildly, and for the information to be passed to me down a telephone line that late at night was frankly very amateurish. The Jockey Club had three full-time members of staff in their press office all day, and at no stage were any newspapers or agencies informed of the official Jockey Club decision. The whole affair was a shambles from start to finish. I just hope that the agony I had to suffer over the affair can be sorted out in future and that no other jockey is messed about by such a farce again.

Dr Turner went to great lengths to tell me that he had spent all day trying to untangle the confusion. The crux of the matter lay in how long I had been unconscious. It's a crazy rule: if I had been out cold for fifty-nine seconds I would have been given a seven-day ban; if I had been unconscious for sixty-one seconds, I would have got twenty-one days. What a joke!

I felt that my ban of twenty-one days was harsh, but it was pointed out that if I had suffered a similar injury in boxing, I would have been stood down for forty-five days.

Dr Toman, who was new to the job at the track and obviously did not know the correct procedure, was quoted as saying, 'I feel very sorry for Tony McCoy because, as he says, he feels perfectly fit, which is why I gave him the minimum ban, but obviously under the rules I'm not allowed to do it.'

I still feel very strongly that I was robbed of a chance of riding in the Grand National. If I was that badly shaken after being unconscious, then surely to God I should have been rushed to hospital for a brain scan, and I should never have been allowed to drive home. If I had suffered a black-out on the way home and wiped out a few cars on the motorway, where would the Jockey Club have stood then? It does not bear thinking about.

I wrote in the *Sun*:

I'm gutted. Being barred from riding in this year's Grand National is one of the biggest disappointments of my life. Less than two weeks ago I was on top of the world after a fantastic Cheltenham Festival, where I landed the two big races on Make A Stand and Mr Mulligan, and on Sunday I was deeply honoured when my riding colleagues voted me the Jump Jockey of the Year at the Lesters awards ceremony. However, it's all gone sour now with the news that I have received a twenty-one day ban and not a ten-day spell on the sidelines. To say I am deflated is a massive understatement. But let's be clear about this. Nothing is as important as the lives of jockeys, so I feel very strongly that the best-qualified man on any racecourse should be the doctor. This whole event makes racing look amateurish. Doctors must know what they are doing before they officiate.

My agent Dave Roberts is right to call for a full Jockey Club enquiry into the circumstances. He's spot on when he says that doctors must be a hundred per cent certain of procedures, but I've got to take it on the chin.

People in charge have made decisions and there's not a lot I can do about it. I feel completely fit and have ridden out six times since the fall. It was a heavy fall but I am fine now.

I accept the rules and understand that they are designed with jockeys' safety in mind, but my biggest disappointment is that the chance to win the Grand National in the same season as winning the Champion Hurdle and Gold Cup has gone. I could be an old-timer before I get that chance again.

But there's no point moaning – life goes on. I'll hopefully have plenty of other years to try and win the Grand National.

*   *   *

John Buckingham said, 'I was disgusted when the doctors changed their ruling and Tony was not allowed to ride in the 1997 Grand National. I know how much he was looking forward to riding in the world's greatest race, particularly after winning the Champion Hurdle and Gold Cup at Cheltenham. To say he was concussed for over three minutes some three weeks before the National was a joke. He'd have been far more on the button than most of the jockeys who took part anyway! The best jockeys should ride in the Grand National, and to deny Tony the chance was completely wrong for him. The public were robbed by his absence. I feel that the stewards often need a ban themselves, the way they hand out suspensions all over the place. They don't realise how much they can cost a top jockey like Tony McCoy when they ban him for three or four days, and don't seem to take into account the potential earning capacity. They ban Tony for a week, like the wrong-course fiasco at Taunton, and give the same sentence to a lesser jockey who will not have as many rides in a week as Tony will miss in one afternoon.

'Tony remains the most dedicated jockey in the weighing-room. I do, indeed, hope to be his valet for the rest of his riding career. My big working ambition now is to hand Tony the winning silks for a Grand National, if only to keep the old Foinavon tradition going. As I say, there's not many days when the 100–1 winner is

Everyone's a winner . . . The Lester Awards winners at the 1996 Oscars ceremony in London. Back (left to right): myself, Sophie Mitchell, Andy Thornton, Dane O'Neill, Richard Johnson. Front: Frankie Dettori, Willie Carson, Jimmy Quinn and Pat Eddery.

Where have you all got to? I look round on Make A Stand at Cheltenham in March, 1997, but there are no dangers on the run-in in the Champion Hurdle.

All smiles . . . I punch the air with delight after Make A Stand has won the 1997 Champion Hurdle. Trainer Martin Pipe is thrilled as he leads in his winner. On the extreme left Martin's assistant Chester Barnes is working out his ante-post winnings, alongside the horse's lad Chris Durham.

The fall and rise of Mr Mulligan. I fall from Mr Mulligan in the King George VI Chase at Kempton on Boxing Day, 1996 at the last fence as One Man strides to victory. However, there are no dangers at the last at Cheltenham as he storms to victory in his next race – the Gold Cup.

Thousands of racegoers pack the Cheltenham Festival stands in 1997 – but there's only one horse in view as I cross the line on fairytale Gold Cup winner Mr Mulligan.

The champagne moment. I celebrate at Ludlow on March 25, 1998 having smashed Peter Scudamore's record with my 222nd winner of the season. Martin Pipe's Petite Risk did the trick for me on my 716th ride

Steady boy! Belmont King makes a complete hash of the last fence in the 1997 Scottish Grand National at Ayr, although that did not stop him winning to round off a fantastic season for me.

Champion, champion! The last day of the season at Stratford in May, 1997. My colleagues are (left to right) Barry Fenton, Richard Dunwoody, Norman Williamson, Jim McCarthy, Mark Richards, Jamie Railton, Andy Thornton, Brendan Powell, Richard Johnson, Sean Curran.

King for a day! The day after my Cheltenham Festival win on Mr Mulligan in the Gold Cup, I'm snapped at Folkestone by the *Sun* on the scales wearing a crown.

Doing a Ravanelli! I pull my vest over my head on the last day of the 1996–7 jump season at Stratford when I was presented with my new Saab, watched by my co-author Claude Duval of the *Sun*.

Not a dry eye in the house: my mother wipes away a tear at my special end-of-season party at Newbury racecourse in June, 1997. This was her first visit to England. On the left is my father Paedar McCoy.

Riding for Martin Pipe is like having your cake and eating it! At my party he presents me with a cake. Watching behind are (left to right) my agent Dave Roberts, my mother, and Mr Mulligan's trainer Noel Chance.

not mentioned. A chap in the army in Yarmouth actually accused me of breaking his leg. He told me that he backed Foinavon at 100–1, went out celebrating, got drunk, tripped on a guy rope and broke his leg. I got the blame!'

*   *   *

My Uttoxeter fall reopened the big debate on whether racecourse medical officers should be appointed under contract to the individual tracks, or be under the jurisdiction of the Jockey Club.

The question was raised after the inquest into Richard Davis's tragic death at Southwell. It was Richard Davis's brother Stephen who pressed for the Jockey Club to appoint doctors, and not racecourses. Britain's fifty-nine racecourses currently use 198 doctors. All but one of them is paid for their work on a daily basis by the racecourse employing them. I would rather see a system where the Jockey Club appoint their own doctors. As I have said, the most important single figure on any track should be the doctor. If the Jockey Club could take responsibility for appointing doctors, the numbers employed would be more than halved and the ability of the individuals given closer scrutiny.

I strongly advocate the idea of recognised pools of doctors covering set areas in the North, Midlands and South. This would involve doctors working regularly with jockeys, and would mean they would understand jockeys' injuries and the rules laid down for injuries and concussion. Ever since Richard Davis's tragic death, this has been a popular suggestion, but the Jockey Club's chief medical officer has treated the idea with caution. Howevers, as Dave Roberts pointed out, 'I am sure the doctor who dealt with Tony will not make the same mistake again, but for instance on Bank Holidays there are sixteen meetings, and another official, just hired for the day, might make the same error.'

Later Dr Michael Turner himself advocated that the Jockey Club should take over control of all doctors employed at tracks. He was obviously keen to avoid another damaging breakdown in communication after the fiasco over my twenty-one-day ban.

At the end of March Dr Turner said, 'We have got to have a centrally regulated system, controlled by the Jockey Club. What we have, has worked very well, with doctors being appointed by individual racecourses, but we are now getting to the stage where every sport is more and more professional. Everything is much more regulated and there is a lot more litigation about. It is reasonable for jockeys to expect doctors on racecourses to be fully clued up, not just with medicine but in the rules of racing.'

Dr Turner admitted that the number of doctors – 198 – was far too many to regulate. He added, 'If we can have a group of doctors who go to a race meeting twice a week, you are talking about part-time officials attending regular meetings and providing a uniform standard right across their parish. I would like to see a fund set up by the Racecourse Association that would take over the finances required to pay all medical staff. I am not saying it will cost racing any more, but it would just be funded differently. Racecourses would pay into a central fund. The average cost of doctors, ambulances and medical staff on a racecourse is approximately £900 a day. We could teach groups of doctors the rules and regulations, and it would be much easier to administer.'

Banned from riding at Aintree, where I would have ridden Paul Nicholls' Belmont King, I was approached by the BBC to be part of their massive Grand National coverage, which is said to have a worldwide audience of 800 million people. It was to be a very special occasion, with that great commentator Peter O'Sullevan due to bow out after his fiftieth and final Grand National. Peter has always been very kind about his reading of my efforts in the saddle. He really is a national institution, and I was delighted when he was made a knight in The Queen's Birthday Honours List in May 1997. No man has done more to convey the thrill of racing to the general public. There must be something special about County Kerry where 'The Voice' was born!

I did several paddock appraisals for the BBC over the three-day meeting, and after Make A Stand had been turned over in the big hurdle race prior to the National, I went into the jockeys' weighing-room to discuss the major form upset with jockey

Chris Maude. Most of the other jockeys were getting ready to ride in the National, and there was the usual pre-race tension. It's odd, but all the normally quiet jockeys jabber away like chatterboxes, and the normally extrovert riders sit as quiet as mice.

I was chatting to Chris Maude and Richard Johnson, who was due to ride Belmont King in my place, when an official told us to vacate the weighing-room immediately. All the jockeys walked out, leaving their belongings behind, items they were not to see for two days.

This was an IRA bomb scare, and within a very short space of time the whole course was cleared. Nobody seemed to panic as I joined most of the jockeys, obviously still in their silks, outside in the main road behind the grandstand.

Luckily I had left my belongings at the Adelphi Hotel, bang in the heart of Liverpool, and eventually I got back there and rebooked my room. Later that evening the Adelphi was full of jockeys still in their riding colours.

The Adelphi has seen some pretty hectic Grand National parties over the years, but I bet that there was nothing to equal this particular one, and Jamie Osborne was well to the fore. One Scouser bumped into him in the bar of the hotel, spotted he was still wearing the colours of Charlie Brooks' Suny Bay and shouted, 'Come straight from work, mate?'

The hotel's disco became quite a nightclub, as jockeys, relieved in a way that they had not been blown to a hundred pieces, really went to town. One actress from the TV soap *EastEnders* was there to enjoy the fun, and I doubt whether she ever dreamt that she would meet such a collection of characters. It certainly beat any night at the Queen Vic.

The hotel agreed that the huge ballroom could be used for sleeping accommodation – at a charge. Russ Garritty, the typical hardman Yorkshire jockey, was having none of that and left. He later said, 'I'm not paying those fancy prices. The missus and I got fixed up reet good on the floor of the Everton leisure centre – for nowt.' It was revealed that jockey David Walsh kindly let twelve jockeys sleep in his bedroom.

The Grand National was rearranged for the Monday, and as I had predicted in my column in the *Sun*, Stan Clarke's Lord Gyllene, a very classy import from New Zealand, was the easy winner at 14–1, beating Suny Bay by twenty-five lengths, with Camelot third under Carl Llewellyn at 100–1. Lord Gyllene became the first horse to make all in winning the National since Troytown in 1920. There is so much about Lord Gyllene to remind me of pictures of Red Rum. He's a very crafty jumper and stays for ever. He's an ideal National horse.

Mick Fitzgerald had caused a bit of a stir the previous year when, after winning on Rough Quest, he said, 'That was better than having sex.'

Tony Dobbin, like myself from Northern Ireland, was shrewd enough to say after winning on Lord Gyllene, 'My girlfriend Vicki is here so I'm not saying that, but it is the best day of my life.'

All the jocks were happy to see Tony Dobbin, who had been 'jocked off' many big-race winners, have his moment of National glory. He's a smashing fella and deserved his success.

However, I raised my eyebrows when I heard Tony Dobbin say about the bomb scare in an interview, 'I'm embarrassed. It is shameful, and it makes you ashamed to say that you come from Ireland, after Saturday's bomb scare wrecked so many people's day out. It never should have happened. Never.'

I agree that the bomb scare should never have happened, but I don't agree that all Irishmen should have to feel ashamed. We are not responsible for the actions of so few. In my opinion there was never going to be a bomb at Aintree, and for one very good reason: there were far too many Irish people there. Probably over a third of the crowd at Liverpool on the Saturday were Irish, and of the thirty-eight jockeys due to ride in the National, twenty were Irish.

It was a terrible blow for the organisers of the race, and incredible that the race was run on Monday in front of a decent crowd. I was asked by Cornelius Lysaght on Radio 5 Live to comment on what a great success it was for Northern Ireland with

Tony Dobbin winning the race. I said simply, 'I'm pleased, of course, for Tony, but nothing can take away the disappointment I feel because I was not allowed by red tape to ride in the race.'

I had a slice of luck that weekend, however. Horses at Aintree were taken over to nearby Haydock Park, while the police and bomb-disposal experts searched every inch of the massive race-course area. Belmont King was one of the very few horses who did not enjoy the drama. He fretted a lot and lost a great deal of weight. Trainer Paul Nicholls was faced with a difficult decision, but he made the right one and pulled Belmont King out of the rearranged Grand National. I am sure that the ground would have been plenty fast enough for him anyway, and he might have kept galloping on, but with the combination of weight loss and fast ground, I don't think he would have beaten Lord Gyllene. Having missed Aintree, Belmont King was able to run in the Scottish Grand National at Ayr exactly a fortnight later.

My big race predictions in the *Sun* had become as accurate as any fortune teller's. The 'They're Off' pull-out had been full of nice, big-priced winners in the Champion Hurdle, Gold Cup and Grand National, but when I got out my pin for the Scottish Grand National my bubble burst.

I was the winner of a £500 free charity bet on any horse in the Ayr marathon after winning the paper's celebrity competition. I was going for a fantastic four-timer and spent hours prior to the race trying to make sure I came up with the right winning selection. I went through the card again and again, and the first horse I discarded was Belmont King. I had walked part of Ayr's course and was quite sure in my mind that the ground was not soft enough for Paul Nicholls' chaser. Finally I opted for Stormtracker as my £500 charity bet . . . only to win the race on Belmont King at 16–1. I therefore did some charity out of a cool £8,000, which was pretty sickening. Stormtracker was pulled up before four fences out.

I got it all wrong with Belmont King. He's a big, heavy horse and I could not see him acting on the officially good ground, but when I walked out to ride Belmont King I could see that Paul

Nicholls had done a magnificent job with him. He looked an absolute picture. Unlike Mr Mulligan before the Cheltenham Gold Cup, Belmont King was the pick of the paddock and looked easily the best turned out.

I was happy to let him bowl along in front, and knew that there were a few disasters going on behind me. Richard Dunwoody was unseated at the fifth fence on the very heavily backed favourite Sister Stephanie, who had come tumbling down from 7–1 to 4–1. Belmont King blundered his way through the twentieth fence and was not too fluent at the last, but still beat Samlee by one and a half lengths.

* * *

Paul Nicholls said after the race, 'Obviously Tony's win on Belmont King in the 1997 Scottish Grand National was a great moment for us all. I gave Tony no orders. I left it all to him and he took the race by the scruff of the neck from the start and was never going to be beaten. He was brilliant and I was so thrilled that I had made the right decision not to run Belmont King at Aintree. I'd love to think that Belmont King will go to the 1998 Grand National with Tony in the saddle.'

Jon Freeman, writing in the *Sunday Times*, summed it up well when he reported, 'A message for anyone who saw an old lady cartwheeling down the streets of Truro last night. Don't call the police and don't imagine they are putting something new in the Cornish pasties. It will have been Mrs Billie Bond celebrating the success of her horse Belmont King in the Stakis Casinos Scottish Grand National at Ayr.'

* * *

It was a fairytale win for Mrs Bond, who sat in front of her television in Cornwall and saw Belmont King achieve his great success. She had made the effort to travel to the ill-fated National at Aintree, but after that disappointment decided not to go to Ayr a fortnight later. The seventy-six-year-old admitted, 'I was laughing, cheering and crying, and drinking whisky – all at the same time.' Mrs Bond suffers from the lung condition emphysema and has great problems travelling too far from Truro. She therefore gave Paul Nicholls strict instructions to buy a horse who would only run on Saturdays, so that she could watch him on television. Belmont King cost 120,000 guineas when Nicholls snapped him up in Ireland in 1994. Mrs Bond is quite a character. Sadly, because of her travelling problems, I have only met her once, when she did make the much shorter trip one day to see us at Newton Abbot. She admits that she is a great cards, roulette and casino fanatic. As a widow, Belmont King has given her a new interest in life.

Much was made of the fact that I was riding my first winner for Paul Nicholls since a double I had for him at Leicester earlier in the year, 14 January, on Korbell (11–4) and Dromhana (100–30). It was hailed as something of a second honeymoon for us after the split with Paul Barber, who was on hand at Ayr and was sporting enough to be the very first to congratulate me when we made our way back to the winners' enclosure.

Paul Nicholls said at Ayr, 'What happened between Tony and me is water under the bridge and I'm glad that he is riding for me again. I know I got a lot of stick for not running Belmont King in the Monday Grand National at Liverpool, but this horse takes a lot out of himself whatever he does, and when he arrived back from the abandoned races that Saturday night he had lost twenty kilos in weight.'

Paul was kind enough to leave all the tactics to me on Belmont King, and I am sure that one day he will run a very big race round Aintree. The bigger the fences, the more he respects them.

Belmont King's win was a welcome change of fortune for Paul Nicholls: the day of the Monday National he suffered the tragedy of his other runner, Straight Talk, being fatally injured.

CHAPTER 13

'You have to be greedy for success while you have the chance'

You may not recognise the mystery guest sportsman who is spraying his new car for the new series of BBC TV's A Question of Sport, which from the autumn of 1997, will be hosted by Sue Barker after David Coleman's long stint as the question master. You will only get glimpses of this particular mystery sportsman, but the gleaming new Saab should be the giveaway for racing fans: it's Tony McCoy washing the vehicle he won as the champion jump jockey at the end of the 1996–7 season.

Three years ago the quietly spoken, lanky lad from County Antrim would not have been recognised by that many people outside the close-knit racing community, but the power of television coverage now means that Tony McCoy has become a well-known figure. Companies such as Blue Thunder Apparel and brewers Guinness are keen to snap up his promotional services. In the autumn of 1996 he also started a weekly column in the Sun's 'They're Off' eight-page racing pull-out.

His Saturday specials soon became a nightmare for the bookies, and Ladbroke's Mike Dillon admitted, 'At one stage we were thinking of closing all our shops on a Saturday. Tony McCoy had a winning streak of tips that seemed to go on and on for ever. As Tony is now firmly established as the favourite jump jockey for millions of betting-shop punters, his opinions are read with great interest. Usually jockeys are the worst tipsters of the lot – they'd have trouble tipping a baby out of a pram – but not McCoy. He's caused us real heartbreak, and if he ever does a Frankie Dettori and goes through the card, the Bank of England will have to print some new notes.'

C.D.

When the *Sun* launched its 'They're Off' eight-page racing section in October 1996, I was signed up to contribute a weekly column. For my first contribution, on 19 October, I reported:

> I've got a cracking first tip to start my debut column in 'They're Off'. Take it from me, General Crack is going to take all the beating in the Charisma Gold Cup Handicap Chase at Kempton today. I can't see him being beaten if he repeats the form of his last race at Chepstow. In that race we got so far clear that when I looked over my shoulder I really thought that all the others must have stopped or fallen. His success was down to owner Paul Barber. When trainer Paul Nicholls' gallops were rock hard after a long dry spell before Chepstow, he arranged for 8,000 gallons of water to be splashed on the ground from water tankers.

Happily, my prediction came true, and General Crack, who had gone up twenty-seven pounds since gaining his first win in a handicap at Wincanton the previous May, duly obliged to get *Sun* punters off to a winning start.

I was lucky enough to strike the following Saturday, when Call Equiname was my main selection in the *Sun* and came out to win the Fred Rimell Memorial Novices' Chase at Worcester. See More Business was due to appear in this race but Paul Nicholls thought that the ground was not quite soft enough. As I predicted in the *Sun*: 'Call Equiname will prove a very able deputy and owes me a win. I was injured three weeks ago at Chepstow after a fall from Iktasab and missed the Call's win in the next race.'

By 2 November 1996, Coral's had suspended betting on the jump jockeys' title. At the start of the summer jumping, David Bridgwater was 10–11 favourite to take the title, despite the fact that I had won it from him by 175–132 the previous season. I was 6–4 second favourite, but when David quit the Martin Pipe job, my odds soon shrunk to 7–1 on, and then in the first week of November Coral's shut up shop when I was just thirty-five winners ahead of David Bridgwater. I wrote in the *Sun*: 'Coral's seem to think I am invincible . . . I just hope that they are right!'

I highlighted another winner in the *Sun* on 9 November when See More Business duly landed the odds on his reappearance in the Rising Stars Novices' Chase at Chepstow. At that stage I wrote:

> See More Business is potentially the best horse I have ever sat on. I rode Viking Flagship to victory at Aintree last season, but I believe that See More Business can go right to the top of the chasing tree. He is making his chasing debut today and it will take something extra special to beat him. Last season I won three hurdle races on him and he looked an absolute cert for Cheltenham, especially after he beat Father Sky by fifteen lengths at Sandown. But then he had heat in his leg and Paul Nicholls and owner Paul Barber decided that it was not worth risking him. Actually it was a minor problem. Don't forget that he is no stranger to fences, as he ran in three point-to-points last year. He won two of them, and it would have been three but for falling at the last in the other one.

See More Business did win his first chase at Chepstow, with *Chaseform* glowing, 'He took to these regulation fences like a duck to water and could hardly have been more impressive.'

On 9 November I was also able to put the *Sun*'s punters on Challenger Du Luc for the following week's Murphy's Gold Cup Chase at Cheltenham. He was then a 12–1 ante-post shot. I advised my readers that Martin Pipe's chaser was thrown in with only 10st 2lb. I had promised Philip Hobbs all along that I would ride Kibreet in the race, after winning at the Cheltenham Festival for the first time in my career on him at the previous season's Grand Annual. I knew that Challenger Du Luc had been schooling brilliantly, but I kept my promise to ride Kibreet, who finished last. Richard Dunwoody produced one of the greatest finishes of the entire season to get up to beat Strong Promise by a head at 7–1. Strong Promise was nineteen pounds out of the handicap.

Bellator kept up my winning sequence of Saturday tips in the *Sun*, when winning the Tote Credit Hurdle at Aintree on 23 November. My housemate Barry Fenton had swept aside the opposition in Bellator's previous race at Wetherby, when the much-fancied Kerawai had been fourth. Bellator was a very easy winner at Aintree, and although hitting the last, won in a canter by fifteen lengths.

I was banned after that ridiculous business with James The First at Newton Abbot on 19 November, when I sustained a three-day whip ban after James The First was pipped by a short head by Jimmy Frost on Well Timed.

Day in day out, we riders get a pretty fair deal from the officials, but I am one who thinks that the employment of professional stewards would greatly enhance the sport. I would far rather have justice dished up by a panel of professional stewards than by the existing amateur officials. An ex-jockey sitting as a professional steward would have a far better grasp of the problems facing a jockey in the hurly-burly of a race than some ex-army major, who has spent the better part of his career in a tank on Salisbury Plain. I was really upset when I received the ban over use of the whip on James The First, and it cost me the chance to ride in the Hennessy at Newbury on 30 November. What riled me about this ban is that James The First, who was then trained by Paul Nicholls, is the biggest dog in racing – bar none. If he was any more of a dog, he'd bark at me! His owners appreciated that he needed a powerful ride, and that's the only way I had won on him before. I'm not a butcher: nobody can ever have accused me of beating up a horse with a whip. At the end of the day all I am trying to do is to win races, and I'd never over-whip an inexperienced horse. However, James The First was different and I'll never forget getting that three-day ban. The stewards claimed that I hit him ten or eleven times, but the last fence of that race was omitted which meant a longer run-in. Even after all this time, the ban still rankles.

I tipped The Grey Monk, but he was no match for ex-hunter chaser Coome Hill, who beat him into second place by four lengths after looking all over the winner for Tony Dobbin. Being banned was no fun, but it meant I was able to school some horses for Martin Pipe and spend a whole day in London opening a pub with Richard Hughes. It was quite an experience for a strict tee-totaller to spend all day in a boozer.

The *Sun*'s readers must have been well pleased with my column on 7 December when the headline read, 'BEL'S TUNING UP FOR WELSH NATIONAL BID'. Belmont King duly came out and won the Rehearsal Limited Handicap Chase at 6–1 at Chepstow. He was running for the first time since April 1995, when he had run second behind Rough Quest at Punchestown. However, he had won a Findus Chase at Leopardstown's Christmas meeting in 1994 and was also very strongly fancied to win the Irish Grand National which was won by Flashing Steel in 1995. Belmont King ran a blinder that day at Chepstow, and was immediately made favourite for the Welsh National after beating Trying Again by one and a half lengths, with a horse called Mr Mulligan back in fourth. It was a good Saturday for me, as I also advised readers to back the other two legs of my treble – Or Royal (5–4) and Bowcliffe Court (5–2).

I greatly enjoyed making my debut at the BBC Sports Personality of the Year Awards in early December 1996. The late-night party afterwards was terrific and I spent so long talking to radio's John Inverdale that the birds were singing when I finally left London and made my way straight down to Newton Abbot for racing the next afternoon. I nearly cleared the BBC's bar out of Diet Coke. John Inverdale was interested in Make A Stand, as he was one of the original five owners, but sadly for him had decided not to come in with Peter Deal when the horse was claimed by Martin Pipe.

The all-night talk with John Inverdale did not seem to do me any harm, and I duly rode a Newton Abbot double on Martin

Pipe's Friendly House and then that old rogue James The First, who owed me a winner. This time James The First, wearing blinkers for the first time over fences, won in good style by twenty-two lengths, and my magic wand was hardly needed.

I was becoming quite a Saturday specialist for the *Sun*, and Go Ballistic was a good tip for me to win the £35,000 Betterwear Cup Chase at Ascot on 21 December 1996. 'MISSING THE PARTY TO HAVE A BALL', screamed the *Sun*'s headline. In the article I revealed, 'All pre-Christmas parties will go out of the window as I sweat like mad to do the ten stone for Go Ballistic. I shall be on a near starvation diet all week to make the weight. But Go Ballistic will be worth it as all his chase wins so far have been at Ascot. It's the first time I have ridden Go Ballistic, but I am confident he'll win.'

Sure enough, the prediction came true and Go Ballistic beat Unguided Missile, from Gordon Richards' Penrith stables, and Scottish-trained Major Bell.

I also teamed up that day with Make A Stand for the first time and took the Mitie Group Kennel Gate Novices' Hurdle. *Chaseform* noted, 'Make A Stand is turning into an extremely useful novice.'

Early January saw bad weather virtually put pay to my bid to beat Peter Scudamore's record of the quickest-ever 150 winners in a season, set on 7 February. By then I was flying with 122 winners, but the arctic blizzards set in and that was that.

In the *Sun* on 4 January I was asked to select my top six for the rest of the 1997 season. I picked out Make A Stand, saying, 'He is the best novice hurdler I have ever sat on when it comes to actual jumping – he simply flies over the obstacles like a seasoned handicapper. Whenever you see him running . . . have a few quid on.' That turned out well, as back then he was 50–1 for the Champion Hurdle he would win in March. I also selected See More Business and Crack On. Mr Mulligan was another of my top six, and I said, 'I am convinced that we have not seen the best of him, and so he is a terrific spare ride to pick up for the Gold Cup.' He was at that time quoted at 20–1 for the Gold Cup.

Belmont King was another of my six to follow in the *Sun*. I said, 'It was very disappointing that the Welsh National was lost to the weather, but on soft ground he could prove the perfect Grand National horse as he stays for ever and ever.' That prediction almost came true. Belmont King was withdrawn from the rear-ranged National, of course, but he duly came out and won the Scottish National.

Just to make sure the *Sun*'s punters got their money's worth, I finally picked Or Royal, and wrote, 'Or Royal won well when wearing blinkers in France, and this could be the key. The ground at Ascot didn't help him and I admit that I came too soon. In blinkers, and held up, I predict that he will win the Arkle Chase at Cheltenham.' Or Royal duly wore blinkers at Cheltenham and won the Arkle Chase, sponsored by Guinness and worth £90,000, at 11–2. I should take over from Mystic Meg after my fortune-telling exploits for the *Sun*.

When the bad weather finally ended, I flew with Richard Johnson and David Walsh to the planned meeting at Mussel-burgh, but when we got to Scotland we found that it had been abandoned. We then discovered that our luggage had been left at Heathrow anyway.

I was back on duty for another Saturday special at Kempton on 18 January when Make A Stand won the Sun King of the Punters Lanzarote Hurdle. He had gone up nine pounds since winning the William Hill Hurdle at Sandown in December, but in the words of *Chaseform*, 'turned another competitive handicap into a mockery, tearing off in front at such a rate of knots that there was no hope for his rivals of living with him. They just had to hope that he would come back to them, but Tony McCoy had no intention of letting them do that and the combination won without being challenged.'

Make A Stand was a good thing that day at 2–1, especially since by using the rules craftily, Martin Pipe had made sure that because of a loophole, four opponents were out of the handicap. Even after this very easy four-lengths win over Gales Cavalier, William Hill still offered 40–1 for Make A Stand for the Champion Hurdle. Looking back, it was the bet of the century.

I suffered two fractured bones in my left shoulder after my fall at Wincanton from Speedy Snapsgem on 23 January and did not ride again until Wednesday, 19 February, when Martin Pipe's Rare Spread was gambled from 5–2 to 9–4 favourite before winning the Lympne Novices' Claiming Hurdle at Folkestone by sixteen lengths. This put me on the 131 winner mark, but my chances of the fastest 150, and of beating Peter Scudamore's record of 221 winners set in 1988–9, were gone.

After that injury, I had spent hours in the Andover Leisure Centre on bikes and in the swimming-pool, plus riding out work for Toby Balding, but I was nowhere like as fit as I thought I'd be, so it was a great feeling to come back with a winner. The comeback win of Rare Spread blew the cobwebs away. I had to pass the course doctor, who had me doing ten press-ups and plenty of other things to prove that I was fit enough to start riding again. The Martin Pipe camp were pleased to have me back, and at Folkestone, Martin's representative Eamonn Leigh told pressmen, 'We have missed Tony and it's good to have him back. Mr Pipe thinks the world of him and he has been more anxious about Tony's fitness than about the horses at the moment.'

I had hoped to keep up my Saturday special winning tips in the *Sun* on 8 March, but Doctoor, who had won his last race so easily for David Walsh at Sandown, got touched off by Carlito Brigante in the Sunderlands Imperial Cup Handicap Hurdle. Doctoor was all the rage in the ante-post lists, and started 3–1 favourite to give the Pipe camp a pre-Cheltenham Festival touch. I led at the second last after holding up Doctoor, but I had no answer to Jamie Osborne and went down by two lengths up the Sandown hill. Jamie was alight at this point of the season, with over twenty winners inside a fortnight.

Earlier that afternoon I had finished second on Belmont King at Chepstow after winning the opener on Potentate. I was also third on Break The Rules – which was rather aptly named – in the two fifteen at Chepstow before dashing off for the 112 mile journey to Sandown. Bob Bray drove my car, with Richard Dunwoody and Charlie Swan in the vehicle as well. The trip took seventy-five minutes, including a stop for petrol! We actually weighed out for the Imperial Cup with two minutes to spare. The other Jockeys thought that I was mean enough to let the petrol go low so that I could make sure of a petrol whipround.

Top sportsmen have often been accused of being mean, none more so than the legendary Lester Piggott. There is an old story of how he was walking along Newmarket High Street one day and saw a wage packet lying beside a shop entrance. He put it quickly in his pocket, but when he got home and counted the money was heard to moan, 'Look at all the tax they have deducted!'

Golf's Severiano Ballesteros was also known to be pretty keen on money. His ex-caddie Peter Coleman tells the story: 'Seve was very difficult to work with in the early days, though he's mellowed a bit now. He used to charge me for golf balls I failed to get back from the practice ground.'

Once, a golf writer was collected by Ballesteros at a Spanish airport in a rusty jalopy of a family car. The writer told him, 'Seve, a star like you should not be seen driving around in a clapped-out heap like this. I can get you fixed up with a sponsored Range Rover for nothing.' The writer kept his word and a new Range Rover was duly delivered to Seve. Six months later Seve met the same writer at a Spanish airport in the same old jalopy. 'What happened to the Range Rover?' the visitor demanded.

'Uses too much petrol,' said Seve, who that very year had banked over £2 million in prize money. You'll never hear me moan about the price of petrol for my sponsored Saab!

It's always nice to receive praise from commentators and pressmen when you ride a winner, and it's especially pleasant when you are praised for riding a horse which finished third. In the *Raceform Update* on 8 March 1997, Lee McKenzie wrote:

Winning jockeys make good jockeys. Whenever a rider is singled out for particular praise, it is odds-on that he or she is the partner of a winning horse. Yet often there is another jockey, further down the field, who has ridden a blinder without anybody noticing.

Tony McCoy gets plenty of plaudits, usually after finishing first yet again, but I was full of admiration for him last Saturday when he came third. The horse was River Mandate, who chased home Turning Trix and Sister Stephanie at Newbury. River Mandate had not finished out of the first two in four previous outings this season, but it was hard to disagree with BBC TV's Richard Pitman when he remarked that the ten-year-old must be an old monkey. From early in the back straight, he had to be coaxed along by McCoy to maintain his lead, and it was only down to the rider that River Mandate managed to hold on to it until the final fence. The champion jockey even managed to conjure up a rally from his partner, and they were narrowly beaten in a head-bobbing finish. McCoy rides loads of winners, but few better than he did here in defeat.

Raceform Update must have been particularly impressed by Lee McKenzie's glowing tribute to me – they printed the identical article twice on the same page!

Gambit's ratings are used by professional punters and book-makers alike. The ratings system was introduced successfully by David de Barrie, an ex-Cambridge University student with a degree in medicine and a flair for figures. He says, 'My ratings are the only ones which take into account the actual jockey who is riding a horse.' Originally, de Barrie studied for an MD at Cambridge's Fitzwilliam College, when he planned a career in medicine, but now it's often the bookies who have to swallow a bitter pill as one of his big-priced selections goes steaming in. He has officially rated me at the top of his jockeys' ratings.

David de Barrie says, 'Backing winners is easy. There are dozens of ways of finding them: following tipsters, methods involving trainers for courses, beaten favourites, and so on. All these will throw up their share of results and I always pay special attention to horses who are ridden by Tony McCoy. Backing winners is easy – backing enough to make the game pay is vastly more difficult. Five years ago in 1992 I decided to forget every-thing I had been told, to start with a clean slate, without preconceptions, and work out what factors were important in the winning of horse races.

'From the start it was obvious that a major consideration, perhaps *the* major consideration, was largely ignored by every professional racing analyst – the jockey. Nobody would doubt that, if there were a match between two novice chasers, both sticky jumpers of the same ability on all known form, but one was ridden by the champion jockey and one by a seven-pound claimer who had never won a race and was unable to claim, you would want to be on the champion – yet no recognised form of race analysis allowed for the merits of the pilot.'

These tables were compiled by David de Barrie. The last column shows his calculated plus factors.

Best averages for the last six seasons

1991–2	P. Scudamore	3.0
1992–3	A. Maguire	3.3
1993–4	R. Dunwoody	3.1
1994–5	R. Dunwoody	2.9
1995–6	A. McCoy	3.8
1996–7	A. McCoy	4.2

Jockeys who have reached +4 on at least one occasion

Jockey	No of times +4	Lowest	Current
A. McCoy	12	0	+4
R. Dunwoody	7	−1	+3
C. Swan	5	0	+2
A. Maguire	4	−2	+2
P. Scudamore	4	−2	Retired
N. Williamson	3	−1	0
J. Osborne	3	−2	+4
G. Bradley	2	−2	+2
R. Garritty	1	−3	+1
L. Wyer	1	−3	+2

* * *

Jim McGrath, form wizard of Channel 4 and *Timeform*, has sung
Tony McCoy's praises, and after Tony won on Most Equal at
Stratford-on-Avon on 9 May 1997 Jim McGrath said, 'That was
the riding performance of the season. Most Equal has to be held
up for a last-gasp challenge, and it was quite incredible the way
Tony McCoy came to win the Needham and James Handicap
Hurdle by a length from Norman Williamson on the favourite
Out On A Promise. McCoy simply lifted the horse over the line.
But from a long way out, while he waited to make his challenge,
there was a certain inevitability about the result. I have never
known any jump jockey ride with the confidence and commitment
of Tony McCoy.'

*   *   *

Bookies were giving little away over my chances of being
champion jockey for the third time in the 1997–8 season. After
our lengthy three-day break at the end of the previous jump
season at Stratford-on-Avon, Ladbroke's made me 'scratch' for
the new season which opened at Perth, and put Adrian Maguire,
Paul Carberry and Jamie Osborne on a start of eighty winners. We
were all priced at 8–1, but having to give away eighty winners
before we have even started seems pretty harsh. After those three
jockeys with a start of eighty, Ladbroke's then quoted Norman
Williamson (90 starts), Richard Dunwoody (100), Tony Dobbin
(120), Richard Johnson (120), Peter Niven (130), Mick Fitzgerald
(135), Russ Garritty (140) and Carl Llewellyn (140).

It's been a wonderful start to my career in England, but a dark
cloud hovered over that tragic meeting at Southwell on 19 July. I
won the opening Fisherton Novices' Handicap Chase on Paul
Kelleway's Sassiver. *Chaseform* were kind enough to note,
'Sassiver did not stride out with any freedom and looked the
least likely to win from some way out, but McCoy is not the
champion for nothing, and backers can thank their lucky stars
that they had him on their side.' I wish the race had never taken
place. It was after his first-fence fall that my popular weighing-
room colleague Richard Davis, who was only twenty, died as the

result of the horrific incident. Tragedies like these are never far away in our dangerous sport, and an accident can strike at any moment during a race meeting.

I was also stunned when Shane Broderick was badly injured on Easter Monday at Fairyhouse in April 1997. Shane, twenty-two, was having his best-ever season, and had finished third on Doran's Pride in the Cheltenham Gold Cup. After riding his thirty-first winner of the season, Royal Oasis, Shane was injured falling from Another Deadly. At the time the fall did not look very serious, but it soon became apparent that Shane was unconscious and urgently needed oxygen. He regained consciousness in Dublin's Mater Hospital, although he was left with paralysing injuries. Shane's fall highlighted the danger that is always lurking.

Richard Dunwoody stepped in for Shane the next day at Fairyhouse and won on Doran's Pride, but Woody readily admitted, 'This is one winner I never wanted to ride.' I felt exactly the same that awful afternoon at Southwell.

Shane Broderick's best friend in the weighing-room in Ireland is Tommy Treacy. Tommy had left Fairyhouse before the fall and said, 'I noticed that police were waiting on the Naas dual carriageway to catch those exceeding the speed limit, so I rang Shane on my mobile phone to warn him to slow down. I couldn't believe it when I was told the news. This is the best friend I have in racing, a very talented jockey – possibly too brave. He never minded himself.'

The luckiest escape from a fall that I've had in my entire career came at Lingfield on 6 March 1996 when it was only thanks to the *Sporting Life*'s photographer Phil Smith that I was not seriously injured. People ask about my worst falls, although I have usually got up and walked away after the most dangerous. It's all luck. However, that day at Lingfield will live with me for ever because the pain was so terrible. I was so fortunate that Phil Smith was standing by the last fence to take his photographs and was able to jump out and come to my rescue. I was riding Brigadier Supreme in the Set Aside Novices' Handicap Chase. It was like a circus rodeo show with fallers all over the place. With all my rivals, bar

one, out of the race, I came to the last fence with a certain victory
in the bag. Brigadier Supreme was so tired, and in any other
circumstances I would have pulled him up. He hardly took off at
the final obstacle and I came crashing down under the horse.
Mark Richards on Fishu was the luckiest winner of the season as
he came from miles back to be the only finisher. He survived all
the carnage and came home alone.

Brigadier Supreme had me well and truly pinned to the deck
and there was no way that I was able to release myself. It was
starting to get very painful indeed and I was finding it very hard to
breathe. I think that I would have passed out if Phil Smith had not
cut under the running rail and rescued me by pulling the horse
away from on top of me.

Phil, one of racing photography's hardest workers, recalls, 'I
shall never forget the screams of agony from Tony as he lay under
that horse. He was really screaming out for his life and I was glad
we were there and able to come to his aid. The horse had virtually
died on top of him and he was completely trapped underneath.
Tony was knackered when we finally released him but he thanked
us and slowly walked away. It was quite remarkable and showed
the courage of these jump jockeys. I was lucky to get a sequence of
eight photographs as the fall took place.'

As I say, the worst-looking falls are sometimes the ones you
walk away from. That one at Lingfield looked awful, and I know
that my parents were watching back in Northern Ireland and
feared something really serious. It's always reassuring for racegoers when they see jockeys declared fit enough to ride in races
after they have had a bad tumble.

I shall never forget the race at Southwell when Richard Davis
died. He started his promising career with Toby Balding and
often used to stay at my old house at Weyhill, when he came
down to ride work. He was a smashing lad and we got on really
well. I won that race and knew that there had been a serious
injury when they dolled off the fence where he had fallen. It was
the saddest day of my life when we learned later that Richard
had died.

Despite all the ghastly falls I have witnessed, and experienced myself, I can honestly say that while riding horses I have never been frightened in my life. Some day I suppose it is inevitable that it will happen, and I'll be scared stiff, but I am better off not thinking about it. The time to quit is when you start to worry about falls.

I made a flying start to the 1997–8 season and broke my own record for the fastest 50 by over a month when Shikaree won the selling hurdle at Newton Abbot on 3 September. My previous fastest 50 came on 9 October 1996.

I readily admit that I am fiercely ambitious to do well, and to ride as many winners as I possibly can every single day. I suppose that I do have an insatiable thirst for winners, and I don't feel that I have to defend my keenness. You have to be greedy for success while you have the chance.

I have seldom missed the opportunity to sneak back to Ireland if I thought there was the chance of a decent winning ride. On 13 July 1997 I popped back across the Irish Sea and rode 12–1 shot Toast The Spreece to win the Guinness Galway Hurdle. It was the first win in the race for Ireland's latest wonder trainer Aidan O'Brien, and for me. Toast The Spreece, who also won the 1997 Irish Lincolnshire, won by half a length from Peter Bowen's raider from Wales, Kinnescash. There were plenty of celebrations afterwards – but not for me, of course – as Toast The Spreece was owned by the Golden Step Racing syndicate, which is headed by Tony Weir of The Step Inn in Stepaside, County Dublin, and Brian Palmer of The Golden Ball in the nearby village of Kilteran.

It was a slightly lucky win for me as Charlie Swan picked the wrong one and went for Aidan O'Brien's other runner, Just Little, who finished eighth.

At Newton Abbot on Wednesday, 5 November 1997, Sam Rockett became the fastest one hundredth winner for me – I went and beat my own record by sixteen days. The year before I had set a new record when I scored winner number 100 at Warwick on 21 November beating Peter Scudamore's old record by thirty days. I felt pretty weak at rainy Newton Abbot that day as I had sweated down to reach my minimum weight of 10st, the first time I had ridden at that weight since the 1997 Cheltenham Festival in March. It had been a fantastic week for me as I rode a double at Plumpton on the Monday, and then a treble at Warwick on the Tuesday.

I arrived at Newton Abbot needing two for the fastest-ever 100 and Bamapour duly obliged in the first race; then Sam Rockett did the trick. Both these winners were for Martin Pipe, who had provided me with 58 out of the century of winners. No sooner had the celebrations died down than I made it 101 on Martin's mare Evangelica.

At that time most racegoers were asking me how I ever won on Martin's Commanche Creek at Warwick that week. I really had to pull out all the stops to win that race. Martin just grinned.

'They're all steering jobs – we were just betting on the distances!' he said. But Martin's bookie-father Dave Pipe had some kind words to say.

'McCoy wins races daily when he's got no right to be in the first three. If I laid McCoy's horses to win in running, when they seemed out of it and down the field, I'd go skint.'

I am not ashamed to want winners every day. You've got to want winners, got to be greedy; but I don't mean being ignorant greedy. When you start winning on Martin Pipe's so-called steering jobs, the appetite for winners just will not go away.

Unfortunately there was no chance of a second Gold Cup triumph for Mr Mulligan, when he had to be retired in December 1997 with a near-fore tendon injury. It was a sad end to a glorious career of twelve wins worth £212,552. I really believe he was good enough to have won a second Cheltenham title.

CHAPTER 14

'I intend to drive myself even harder'

The scene could hardly have been more dismal. Newton Abbot's tiny Devon track was all gloom and doom as relentless rain lashed the course on 3 September, 1997. Caterers were scurrying into the stands around ten o'clock as a blue Saab was the first vehicle to purr to a halt in the members' car park. The identity of the passenger would have been an easy one for A Question of Sport – the champion jump jockey Tony McCoy. Crumpled-up copies of the Racing Post *and the* Sun *lay at his feet, and a pillow left in the passenger seat would have been an obvious clue as to the remarkable record-breaking lifestyle of the young Irishman. However, this was yet another day when McCoy was to gallop relentlessly into the record books and show a steely drive which would leave lesser men collapsing with exhaustion.*

Driven to the course by Nick Jackson – later to be Walter Swinburn's agent – McCoy dashed straight to the weighing-room and started with a hot bath. He then endured over one hour in the sauna bath, his only intake the luxury of the odd sip of water. This is the hard side of McCoy's life that the public never sees. It was one of the coldest and most unpleasant days of the autumn, and McCoy confided in a brief awakening in the car, between dozing on the pillow, 'I feel knackered . . . and I've also got flu.'

Sweating in a sauna and then going out into the bitter, slanting rain with flu would have caused most sportsmen to go as weak as a kitten, but we were about to see yet more McCoy magic unfold.

At the start of the meeting at Newton Abbot McCoy's score was on 47 wins. He had five rides, and the few national newspapermen who had made the long haul to Devon were very much hoping that the champion jockey would oblige with the fastest ever 50 in the history of jumping. We were not to be disappointed.

McCoy was on Marsayas in the aptly named Alice in Wonderland Novices' Hurdle. This is the wonderland of McCoy, and he was seen at his forceful best as he got the 11–8 on favourite to win in the dying strides by half a length. His small horse was never going well and hated absolutely every inch of the rain-softened turf. Few other jockeys, apart from McCoy, would have won on him.

Martin Pipe's bookie father Dave was as usual by the winner's enclosure to greet McCoy. He beamed: 'Just how many more races is AP going to pull out of the bag? I'd have gone skint years ago if I had laid horses ridden by AP in running. Sometimes he looks certain to get beat – more likely to get tailed off – and he still comes and does 'em.'

Winner number 49 came when Martin Pipe's Running de Cerisy stormed home in the next race by 11 lengths. In the third race McCoy was at the rear of the field on Pipe's Shikaree, when he suddenly moved into top gear and came with a lovely smooth run to win by an effortless 18 lengths. Waiting hacks' and photographers' early rise was not to be in vain. McCoy had ridden the fastest ever 50 winners in a season and had smashed his own record by over a month. The previous season he had waited until 9 October to record the fastest 50. Shikaree was 32lb well in with his rivals but as Pipe said, 'Every winner is a winner. They all count.'

With a touch of mischief the champion trainer added, 'These McCoy winners are all steering jobs. We are just betting on the distance!'

I reported this lighthearted remark in the Sun, but sadly the Sporting Life – in its death throes – took it seriously and attempted a follow-up by quizzing Pipe as to whether his team *actually instructed McCoy to win by certain distances, which had become a popular part of spread betting.*

Sipping a celebration Diet Coke, McCoy fielded questions from journalists in the small weighing-room. 'It's the same as usual. I shall try and beat all my records, and the big one is Peter Scudamore's remarkable best-ever season score of 221. It will be a hell of a task and I shall have to stay injury free. But all the time Martin Pipe is supplying easy winners like that, I shall have a chance.'

Amongst all the cameras clicking, and Pipe's mobile phone proving yet again the slogan that 'It's good to talk', few could have envisaged the actual sweat that goes into the McCoy winners' machine.

However, this was only one small milestone in McCoy's best-ever season: the fastest 50 became the fastest 100, then the fastest 200, overhauling the great Scu's 221, and at the end of his season – cut short by a freak injury – McCoy had hoisted 253 winners. Surely that score will never be beaten.

McCoy assured me, 'I know that I can beat that total. People are always telling me that I should take my foot off the pedal and take things a bit more easily, but I have no intention of doing that. In fact I intend to drive myself even harder.' We truly are watching jumping's greatest ever phenomenon.

Jim 'Crocodile' McGrath, BBC TV's brilliant commentator, who has taken over from Sir Peter O'Sullevan as 'the Voice of Racing', said, 'In a planning meeting for Grandstand I stressed to directors and producers that on most Saturdays McCoy was riding at our main meetings, which we are covering. I impressed on them that in McCoy our viewers are not only watching the best jump jockey in the world, but also the greatest ever.' Few would disagree.

C.D.

B reaking Peter Scudamore's record of 221 winners in a season was the obvious highlight of my 1997–8 campaign, and I was thrilled to hoist my total to 253 before a freak fall put me out of action. Records seemed to tumble down like tenpins and the whole season went along at such a tremendous pace that I was hardly able to keep up with it myself.

Having been crowned champion of the previous season at Stratford-on-Avon, I had just seven days out of the winner's enclosure before Ordog Mor opened my new account at Southwell on 7 June. They say there is no rest for the wicked, and that's certainly the case with jump jockeys. The old season ends on a Saturday and the new one starts on the next Thursday – or even sooner. Summer jumping has transformed the picture and all new records must now take that into account.

I smashed my own record for the fastest 50 ever when Shikaree won at 7–4 on for Martin Pipe at Newton Abbot on 3 September. I don't suppose the Devon track had ever seen so many photographers there before, and it was a very happy occasion. I had flu and had been sweating like mad before racing, and I was glad to get that particular milestone out of the way.

The previous season all my wildest dreams had come true when Make A Stand had made all to win the Champion Hurdle at the big Cheltenham Festival and Mr Mulligan had pulled off a shock win in the Gold Cup. Now by a cruel twist of fate both these brilliant horses had been wiped completely out for the season.

Mr Mulligan ran a blinder for me when trying to give away nearly a stone to Gales Cavalier on his reappearance at Wincanton in October. Timeform's much-respected Jim McGrath told me after the race that he thought it was the best race Mr Mulligan had ever run. A second Gold Cup win looked very much on the cards and Mr Mulligan went on to score for Richard Dunwoody at Ayr. However, an injury meant the end of his career. He was a fine, big chaser, and if I live to be a hundred years old I will never forget the thrill of him charging up the hill at Cheltenham and flying the last fence with the Gold Cup in the bag. Great memories.

Make A Stand picked up an injury when he was defeated at

Aintree the previous spring and Martin Pipe ruled him out for the season but hoped that he would return one day to defend his Champion Hurdle crown.

I recorded the fastest ever 100 when Sam Rockett won at Newton Abbot on 5 November. I had earlier scored on Martin Pipe's Bamapour. I had beaten my own previous record by 16 days. The previous season I had become a ton-up kid at Warwick on 21 November, shattering Peter Scudamore's previous best by 30 days. Reaching the fastest 100 on 5 November was certainly one Guy Fawkes Day I'll never forget – Rockett man included! It was quite a week for me as I rode a double at Plumpton on the Monday and a treble at Warwick on the Tuesday.

As usual Martin's father Dave Pipe was there to witness my wins and he told pressmen at Newton Abbot, 'McCoy wins races daily when he's got no right to be in the first three. Both Bamapour and Sam Rockett looked well cooked . . . yet they still won.'

Press photographers asked me to smile and give a thumbs-up when I came back to the winner's enclosure, but it was all I could do to smile – I felt like death, completely drained. My alarm had gone off at six that morning, and I had had my usual hour in a scalding-hot bath before I dashed down to Martin Pipe's to school some of his new arrivals from the flat-racing world.

I had slept most of the way to Newton Abbot, with Nick Jackson at the wheel, then had had another hour or more in the racecourse sauna. That day I had been asked by Martin Pipe to do my very minimum of 10 stone on the mare Evangelica. I told him I'd make the weight and I was determined not to put up any overweight. Many people thought that I was greatly endangering my health by sweating down to 10 stone, and I was urged to resist the Martin Pipe lightweights. Many of my colleagues saw me sweating away on a horrible, overcast and rainy day and thought that I had gone off my head. I admit that my face was as white as a sheet and I looked very lined. Raising those smiles was quite an effort. Happily, Evangelica won her three-horse race with the 11–8 on favourite General Crack tiring going to the last and I was able to score easily.

I had suffered from a cold for months and couldn't throw it off. Sweating and then going out into the cold winter weather obviously didn't help. Many see Martin Pipe as a kind of Svengali, orchestrating my every move, but it's not like that. I'm not under any pressure from the champion trainer to get down to these low weights. I don't regard it as a health hazard. I'm really under no pressure from Martin Pipe and I take these decisions off my own back.

Nick Jackson could see that behind all the excitement of the fastest 100 I was really suffering. He told me, 'You are 6lbs better than any other jockey, so why the hell don't you tell trainers that you will ride these lightweights . . . but you'll put up overweight.'

It's a nice idea, but if you are a true professional you must make the weights that you have agreed to ride at. In the 1997–8 season three times I wasted and sweated down to ride at 10 stone. Evangelica won for me that day at Newton Abbot, but Loveufrank fell at Cheltenham and then I got beaten on another one in a Bangor seller.

Nick Jackson drove me home from Devon that night and we stopped at our usual spot for a meal . . . a motorway garage to buy a few tins of Diet Coke, a packet of crisps and some Jaffa Cakes.

I honestly have no fear of anything in the saddle. I have never been scared for one second on a horse. I have no fear of anything . . . except putting on weight. It is the daily fear all jockeys suffer from, and being nearly six foot tall it is a constant battle. I often dream about a big meal of roast chicken and roast potatoes. I love chocolate puddings, too. But it is all a dream. I accept that eating the odd bar of chocolate to get energy is not a good idea, but when you are dashing around the country, having a proper balanced diet is not easy.

Like a lot of Taureans, I am very stubborn. If I have to go a day without a meal, I'll do it. I refuse to be beaten and I'm also very superstitious. I hate passing anybody on the stairs. If I have three big dislikes it is slow drivers on the roads, drink and cigarettes. While I dislike being passed on the stairs I also dislike being passed near the winning-post. Happily, in the 1997–8 campaign that did not happen too often in tight finishes.

I recorded the fastest-ever 150 winners in a season when Jymjam Johnny won at Bangor on 17 December. This was one of the few winners I have ridden for Jonjo O'Neill, who was a great champion jump jockey in his time before switching to training.

Everything was now set for the King George VI Chase at Kempton on Boxing Day. It looked a fantastic race and I teamed up with Martin Pipe's highly talented Challenger du Luc. I had already finished second on him twice before the King George VI and knew all about his quirks. As Martin told me, 'This horse has more A levels than the rest of the horses in my yard put together. That's his trouble, he's too damned clever.'

At Newbury when I got beaten on Challenger du Luc by Callisoe Bay I let him go to the front pulling a train, only for him to turn it in, and I lost on the evens favourite by a head. I could have cried. However, that was nothing to the heartbreaks this customer had in store for me.

Challenger du Luc ran a blinder when second to Senor El Betrutti in the Tripleprint Gold Cup at Cheltenham and I really fancied that Kempton would suit him well. He was 16–1 and I know that Martin Pipe advised owner David Johnson and everybody to 'get on'.

I jumped the last fence alongside See More Business and I don't think I have ever been more confident of winning a race. I had tons up my sleeve and it was simply a case of when I pressed the button. He was almost laughing at Paul Nicholls' fine chaser, who had been one of my favourites when I rode for the Somerset trainer. But when I let down Challenger du Luc, he blatantly didn't try an inch and in the end See More Business beat us by two lengths. I don't know who Challenger du Luc was breaking up more – me or his unlucky owner. I could not have produced him any later in the race and he still turned it in.

Even at that stage, and with all the frustrations, everybody was telling me that Challenger du Luc was just the kind of odd individual to win the Grand National. I didn't know whether to laugh or cry! However, it was true that horses like Last Suspect and Maori Venture did show their very best form when taking on the most feared fences in the world to win the National.

My riding was being kindly received by the national newspaper writers. Robert Philip in the *Daily Telegraph* wrote, 'The clumsiest carthorse will be persuaded to soar like Pegasus in the hands of Tony McCoy.' In the *Sunday Telegraph*, after my life story was first published, Brough Scott reported, 'Watch Tony McCoy and wince. Never in jump racing's long, thundering history has anybody galloped so fast towards the record books as this tall, lean, white-faced twenty-three-year-old. And never have the fences looked so certain to get their man. McCoy admits, "It's a hard game, so it is."'

The fastest-ever 200 came when Martin Pipe's Fatalise won at Kempton on 28 February, 1998. It was a typical steering job for the champion trainer and I beat Peter Scudamore's record which he had set on 27 April, 1989. Peter was always the very first to congratulate me, and I must point out that I did have the advantage of summer jumping. But I was able to record the double ton 59 days quicker. It was already being said that I was odds-on to pass Scu's career total of 1,678 winners. That took Peter 16 seasons, while I was only in my fourth season.

At that stage Hills quoted me at 10–1 to reach an incredible 300 winners in the season. I never fancied myself for the 300. Hills must have thought that I was some kind of robot. It meant that I'd have to average eight winners a week right through to the end of May. I set my sights on 250. To take me to the magic 200, I had ridden 122 winners for M. C. Pipe.

The 300 was never on when I sustained the odd injury – and whip ban – which put me on the sidelines for a few days. Much fuss was made when it was revealed that the Jockey Club's Malcolm Wallace had privately written to me warning me about my whip action. Many thought that this smelt of a secret court. I took the view that it was far better to get a warning letter than actually be stood down for a few days. I had been quizzed over the use of my whip in one driving finish, but I pointed out that I had been riding a proven 'dog', and as the horse had started 2–1 on favourite I would have been lynched by punters if I had not done my best to win. I was also able to point out that I had never marked a horse with a whip in my life.

My dreams of retaining my Cheltenham titles with Make A Stand and Mr Mulligan had both been dashed in different ways for the 1998 Festival meeting, but I felt sure that I was going to have a successful meeting. The previous year I had been top jockey with three wins – Or Royal, Make A Stand and Mr Mulligan. Now I was to take that title for the second successive year with five winners, two seconds and two fourths from my sixteen rides. I had won £241,801 for my lucky owners . . . and my own ten per cent wasn't too bad for three days' work!

Jockeys, of course, aren't allowed to bet, but I told all my owners, friends and millions of *Sun* readers via my column that I was very confident I would win all the last three races on the Festival card. Luckily, that's exactly what happened and I won the Grand Annual on Edredon Bleu for Henrietta Knight, the Cathcart on Cyfor Malta and the County Hurdle on Blowing Wind. I had told everybody that Edredon Bleu was my banker of the meeting.

Winning the Arkle Chase on Champleve gave me the greatest pleasure of the season up to that stage. I'd won it the year before on Or Royal and it is never an easy race to win. Champleve was only five years old but he jumped the second last like a stag and just held on to win by a short head. Beating Richard Dunwoody on the runner-up Hill Society really capped it all for me. I shall never tire of beating Woody in close finishes.

With Unsinkable Boxer winning the Gold Card Hurdle Final by four lengths it was a great meeting for Martin Pipe. Unsinkable Boxer, who had only won novice races prior to this, landed some really heavy gambles down to 5–2 favourite.

I got rave reviews for winning on Edredon Bleu as I made all and ran the rivals ragged, just managing to get him home as he tired. Cyfor Malta was very different and had to be held up.

Blowing Wind was red-hot 15–8 favourite and all of Cheltenham seemed to be cheering him home in the last-race gloom. He picked up a £50,000 bonus for happy connections as he had previously won the Imperial Cup just recently before at Sandown. He had to work harder than he had four days before but it was typical Pipe magic.

My prediction of winning the last three races had come true and my happy fans were stuffing wads of 'readies' into their pockets. It took me for ever to get away from the track. I was swamped by autograph hunters – many of them fellow Irishmen – and I really felt like a Celtic footballer as I signed away on punters' racecards.

I missed the previous Grand National meeting over my controversial 'unconscious' ban, but I made up for it this time and was top jockey with five winners. I had been top jockey in 1996 with three successes. This time I won on Fataliste in the Seagram Top Novices' Hurdle, Cyfor Malta in the John Hughes Trophy Chase, Boss Doyle in the Mumm Mildmay Novices' Chase and Unsinkable Boxer in the Belle Epoque Sefton Novices' Hurdle on the first two days. I was able to receive my award prior to racing on the Saturday, as by then nobody could catch me.

Saturday, 4 April, 1998 is a day I will never forget. If I am asked the greatest riding feat of my career I will answer: Pridwell winning the Martell Aintree Hurdle. The worst moment of my career: getting a six-day ban for excessive use of the whip during that race! I punched the air with delight when I won on Pridwell, beating my great Irish rival Charlie Swan on the Champion Hurdler Istabraq by a head. Istabraq was 7–4 on favourite and Pridwell was 6–1.

I could not believe it when I got a four-day ban, extended to six when I appealed. It was a disgraceful decision. The horse was not marked and everybody knows that Pridwell is no battler. I had beaten the Champion Hurdler in an £80,000 race and got kicked out for six days. Anyone could see that I was not flogging a dead horse. Pridwell. who had been fourth previously behind Istabraq in the Champion Hurdle, responded bravely to all my urgings. I can only think that the stewards were influenced by the fact that millions were watching this race round the world, prior to the Grand National.

Challenger du Luc was my National ride. I felt, like Martin Pipe, that Aintree might bring out the best in this old so-and-so. He is such an enigmatic customer and it would have been fascinating to see how he jumped round Liverpool. However, we shall never know – he fell at the very first fence and sent me flying.

That evening I went to a farewell dinner for popular retiring jump jockey Mark Dwyer in York. It was a fantastic turn-out of the jumping fraternity. I still kept on about the Pridwell ban, and obviously my pride had been dented when Challenger du Luc ditched me at the very first fence in the Grand National. I had a face like thunder all evening, and only smiled near the end of the meal when BBC radio's Cornelius Lysaght, who was at my table, shouted across, 'There's a prize for the most miserable man in the room and you are 6–1 on to win, AP – even without a whip!' I had to smile when he said that, but inwardly I was still very hurt.

My next big target was to pass Peter Scudamore's best-ever season total of 221, set in 1988–9. A double on Lannakaran and Pomme Secret equalled the record at Chepstow on 24 March. I equalled Scu's record on my 710th ride of the season, whereas Scu took 663 rides, achieving the feat on Hazy Sunset at Stratford on 3 June, 1989. I beat the record the next day on Petite Risk at Ludlow and soaked everybody in sight with champagne like a Formula 1 Grand Prix winner. It took me 49 rides more than Scu, but I did it in 296 days, whereas Scu took 309. I do not relish all the press attention and I honestly was very glad when it was all out of the way. It meant that I had won on thirty-one per cent of my rides. John Francome was very kind and said, 'Tony McCoy is not only the fittest jockey I have ever seen – he's the greatest.'

My career total stood at 666. I took my season's total to 253 and was keen to beat Sir Gordon Richards' record of 269 winners in a season. However, that all ended when I agreed to ride the top Irish hurdler-chaser Derrymoyle for trainer Michael Cunningham in the Marlborough Cup on Sunday, 24 May. We got as far as the fourth obstacle and that was that. I crushed a vertebra in the fall at the timber fences. I was out for the rest of the season and the score of 253 goes into the record books. But for that back injury who knows what I might have achieved.

Many thought I was mad to take the ride over timber fences, but Derrymoyle was favourite for a £50,000 race and I don't regret it. I would not have taken the ride in March, however, with Cheltenham and Aintree coming up. Before the Derrymoyle fall I was also top jockey at the Punchestown Festival with four wins, including one on His Song, whom I rate as potentially the best horse I have ridden recently.

The 1997–8 season was great for me, and Martin Pipe was brilliant. He's completely blinkered and only thinks of training winners. That's all that's on his mind. Even if he has four wins in an afternoon, he's only interested in winning a fifth race.

One of the proudest moments of my career came in March, 1998 when I was voted Jockey of the Year in a poll of my fellow riders. I beat a six-strong field of nominations, which included Richard Dunwoody and the very popular Frankie Dettori. Getting the winning vote actually ended a run of three wins by Frankie. Although I won the Jump Jockey of the Year award for the second successive season, I became the first rider from the jumping game to win the overall Jockey of the Year award. Not even Richard Dunwoody, who had won five of the jump jockey titles in the eight years of the Jockeys' Association awards ceremony, had managed to pull off the double.

To break the stranglehold of Frankie Dettori was a great thrill. It's quite something when you are recognised by your own profession at the Lesters awards, which is racing's equivalent of the Oscars in showbusiness. I suppose winning both the Champion Hurdle on Make A Stand and the Gold Cup on Mr Mulligan at Cheltenham in 1997 helped clinch the title.

My then housemate Barry Fenton won the Conditional Jockey of the Year award so there were two Lesters prizes under the one roof that night, or rather the next day when we finally got home.

Jumping is like a game of snakes and ladders, with its ups and downs. I suffered disappointments, like when Cyborgo ran out in the Gold Cup at Cheltenham, but Pridwell's win at Aintree put me on a superb high, until the six-day ban. Challenger du Luc broke my heart. I've never won on him and I've promised David Johnson that one day I will win a big race on him. Having had three unsuccessful tries in the Grand National, the Aintree thriller is the one big race I would dearly love to win.

I admit that I am obsessed by winning. I make no apologies. However, I am no head-down, eyes-shut horse-flogger. Martin Pipe says that I don't know when I'm beaten. Mind you, he says that most of his winners are steering jobs and he could make a comeback and win on most of them!

I believe my total of 253 can be beaten, and I'm going to have a real good try. You don't last in this bone-crunching game for ever, so I'm determined to make the very most of it while I can.

Index